11+
Non-verbal Reasoning

WORKBOOK 2

Non-verbal Reasoning Technique

Dr Stephen C Curran
with Andrea Richardson
Edited by Katrina MacKay

This book belongs to

Accelerated Education Publications Ltd

Contents

6. Components   Pages
1. Key Questions in NVR   3
2. Elimination Skills   3
3. Descriptive Skills   3-4

7. Odd One Out
1. Basic Level   5-7

8. Codes
1. Type 1 - Level Two   8-10
2. Type 2 - Level Two   11-13

9. Analogies
1. Level One   14-16
2. Level Two   17-19

10. Similarities
1. Level One   20-22
2. Level Two   23-25

11. Series   Pages
1. Level One   26-28
2. Level Two   29-31

12. Matrices
1. Level One   32-34
2. Level Two   35-37

13. Revision
1. Odd One Out   38-39
2. Codes   40-41
3. Analogies   42-43
4. Similarities   44-45
5. Series   46-47
6. Matrices   48-49

Chapter Six
COMPONENTS

The **Components** of Non-verbal Reasoning comprise:
Key Questions • **Elimination Skills** • **Descriptive Skills**

1. Key Questions in NVR

All NVR questions are centred around three key areas:
1) The shape most **Similar** 2) The shape most **Different**
3) The next shape in a **Series** of shapes (identify a pattern).

2. Elimination Skills

Eliminating the wrong options one by one, by marking them or crossing them out, helps to identify the answer.

Example: Which shape is most like the Test Shape?

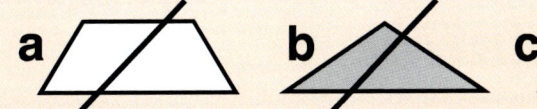
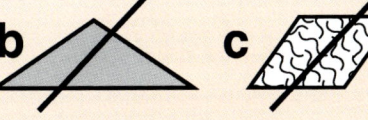

Test Shape

Answer: **d** - It is four-sided and has a Grey Fill.

3. Descriptive Skills

Descriptive Skills in Non-verbal Reasoning aid understanding. A summary of descriptive skills is given below:
Elements • **Movements** • **Manipulations** • **Patterns** • **Layering**

a. Elements
(i) Shapes

Standard Shapes comprise all 'closed' geometrically defined shapes.

Rectangle

Specialist Shapes comprise everyday recognisable 'closed' shapes.

Boat

(ii) Fills

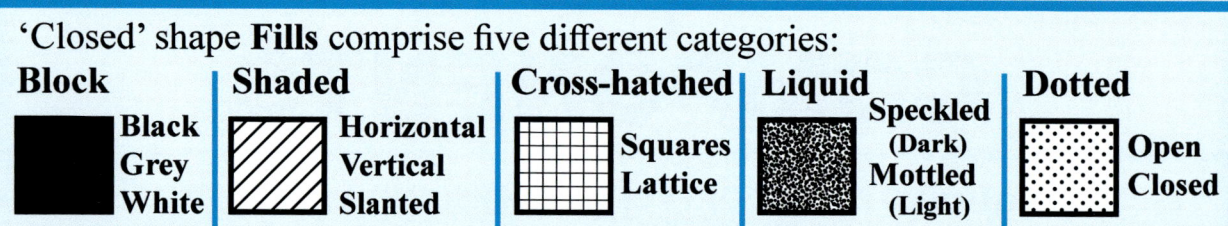

(iii) Lines

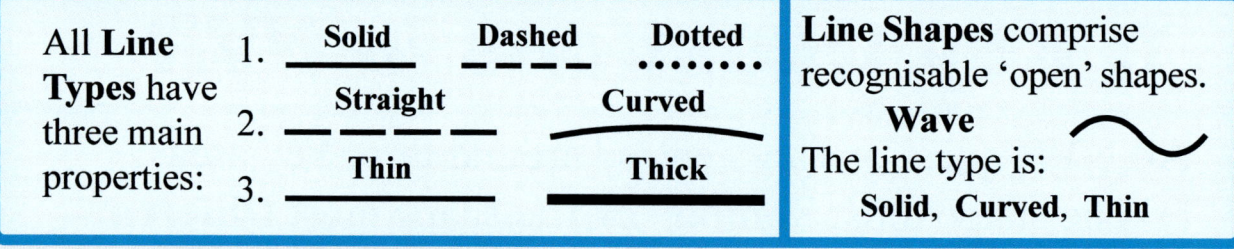

b. Movements

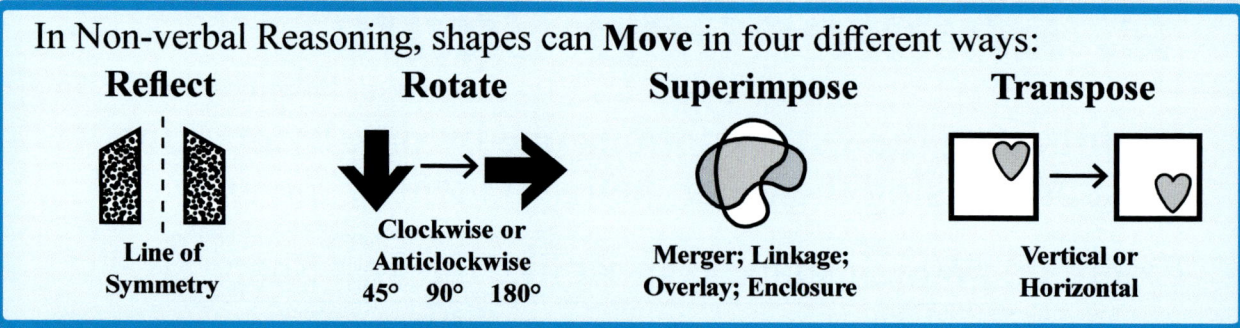

c. Manipulations

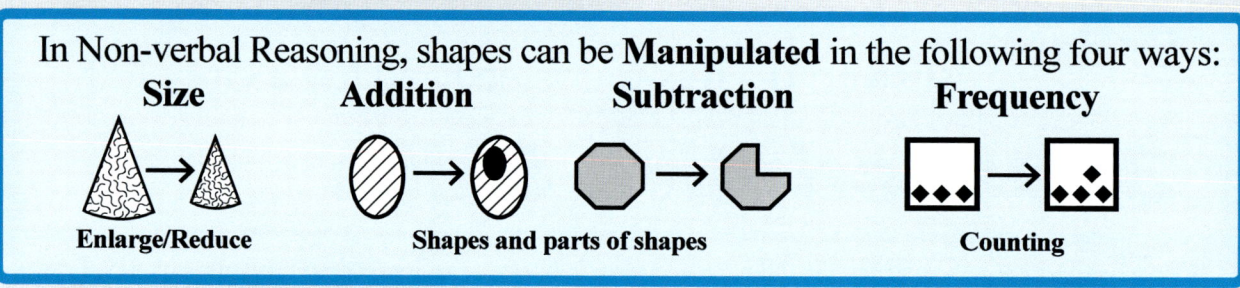

d. Patterns

In Non-verbal Reasoning, shapes can make **Patterns** in two different ways:

Repetition ⇐ ⇓ ⇒ ⇑ ⇐   **Cumulation** ⬡ ⬡ ⬡ ⬡

e. Layering

Layering occurs when changes to shapes or figures are combined. Questions with up to five layers or changes can seem complex. **This book involves learning to identify & describe these layers.**

Chapter Seven
ODD ONE OUT

In Verbal Reasoning, choosing the **Odd One Out** involves seeing how the meaning of each word in a group of words relates to the other words.

Example:

In this group of five words, three of the words are related in some way and two are not. They are the odd ones out.

    ash   **branch**   oak   **leaf**   willow

branch and **leaf** are odd ones out as they are not tree types.

In Non-verbal Reasoning, choosing the odd one out involves spotting which likeness links a group of shapes and identifying which shape does not have this likeness.

Example:

All the shapes have four sides except the Triangle which only has three sides, so this is the odd one out.

1. Basic Level

Odd one out questions only ever operate at Level One. This means there is only one layer or change to look for. On easier questions this can be spotted very quickly.

Example: Which shape is most unlike the others?

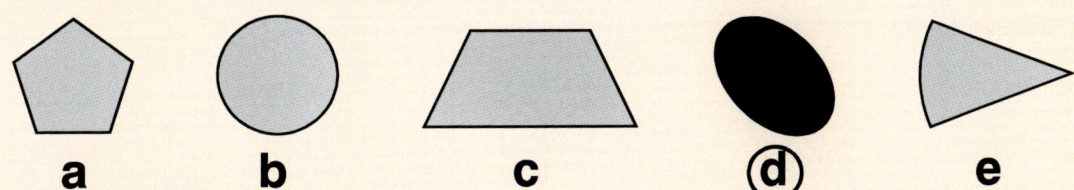

   a   b   c   ⓓ   e

Answer: **d**

All the shapes have a Grey Fill except the Ellipse, which has a Black Fill, making it the odd one out.

Exercise 7: 1 Which figure is the odd one out?

1) 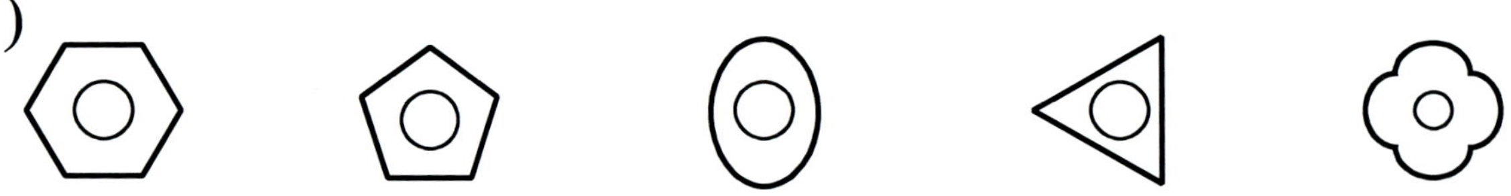
   a   b   c   d   e

   Why? *The Circle is not the same size as the other Circles.*   Answer ____

2) 
   a   b   c   d   e

   Why? _____ Answer ____

3) 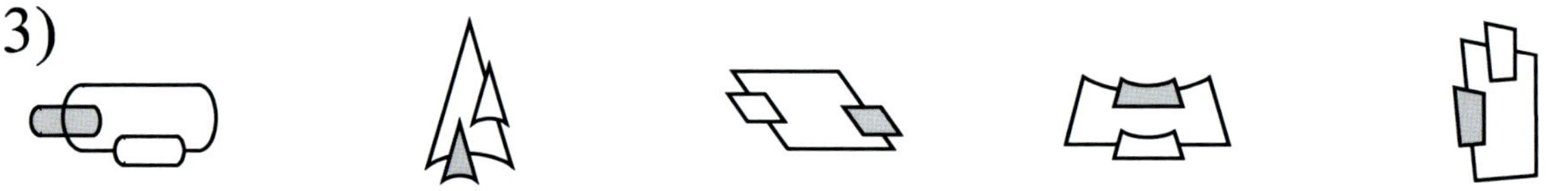
   a   b   c   d   e

   Why? _____ Answer ____

4) 
   a   b   c   d   e

   Why? _____ Answer ____

5) 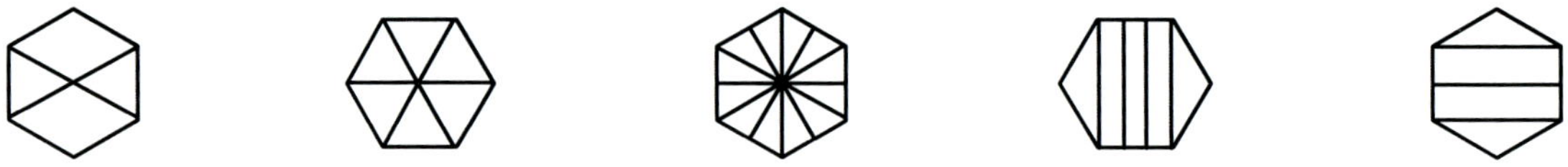
   a   b   c   d   e

   Why? _____ Answer ____

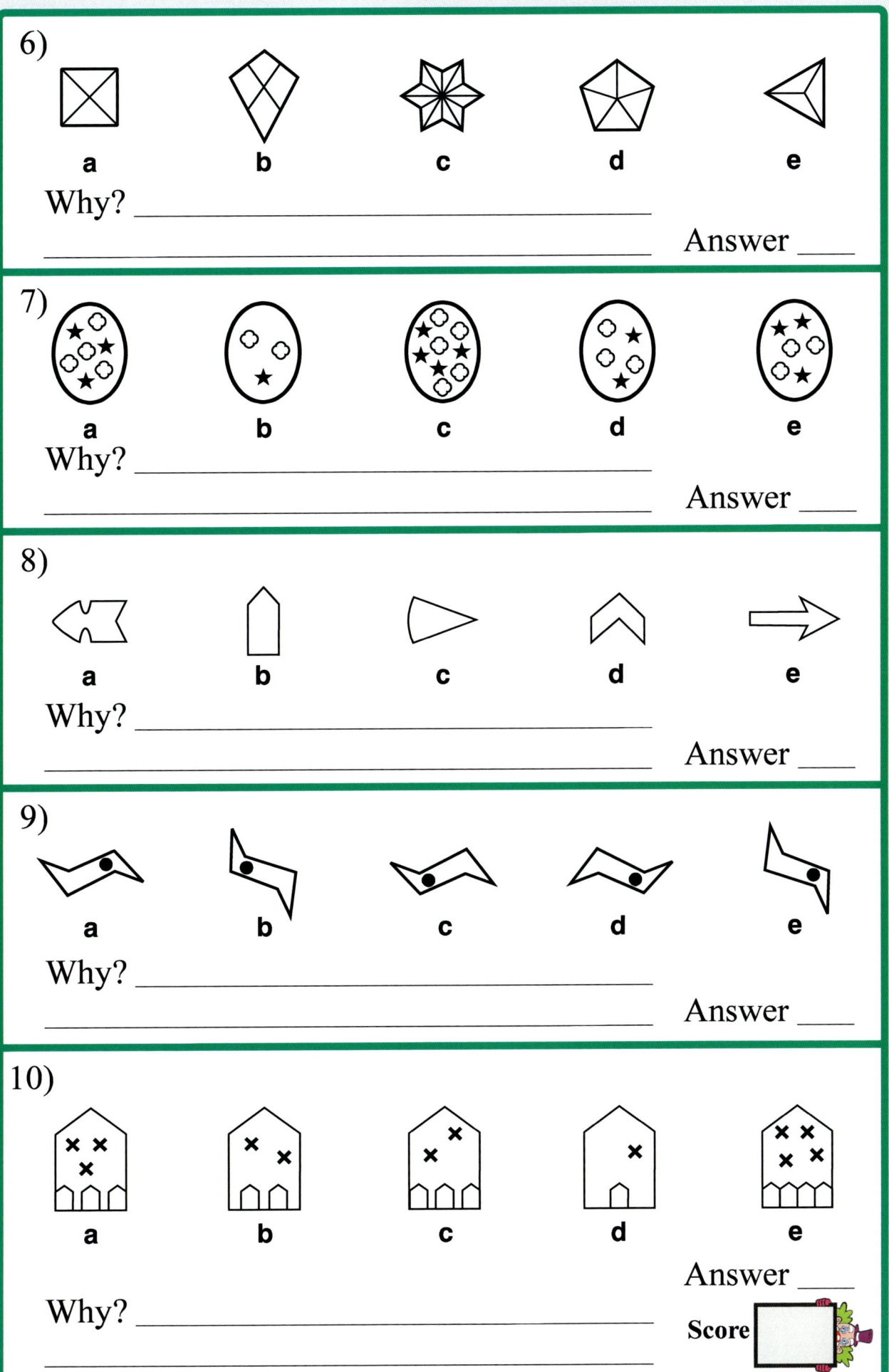

Chapter Eight
CODES

The skill of **Decoding** in Verbal Reasoning involves finding out what the letters or numbers represent.
For example: If **678** means **PIT**, what does **876** mean?
Each digit represents a letter. Answer: **TIP**
In Non-verbal Reasoning, letters are often used to represent:
Shapes • **Fills** • **Lines**

1. Type 1 - Level Two

Decoding in Non-verbal Reasoning involves working out which letters go with which shapes. A **Level Two** code question has two letters which represent the correct shape. Level One (one letter) questions are too easy for tests.

Example: Which pair of letters represents the Test Figure?

MA
MB   Test Figure   NB   MB   MC   AM   NA
                    a   b   c   d   e
NC

The Code Rules are as follows:
Layer One - **M** stands for Square; **N** stands for Triangle.
Layer Two - **A** stands for a White Fill; **B** for a Grey Fill; **C** for a Black Fill.

N̶B̶   M̶B̶   MC   A̶M̶   N̶A̶
 a   b   c   d   e

It is important to **eliminate** the wrong possibilities:
a and **e** - **NB** and **NA** are incorrect because they stand for Triangles.
b - **MB** is incorrect because **B** stands for a Grey Fill.
d - **AM** is incorrect because **A** stands for a White Fill and the letters are not in the correct order, which is not permitted.

Answer: **c** - **M** stands for Square; **C** stands for a Black Fill.

Exercise 8: 1 Which pair of letters on the right represents the Test Figure?

1)   DY / DZ / EY   Test Figure

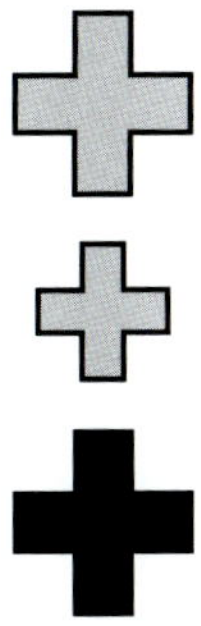

YD	ED	YE	EZ	DE
a	b	c	d	e

Answer ____

Code Rules:
i) D - Grey Fill; E - Black Fill.
ii) Y - Large Cross; Z - Small Cross.

2) SP / SQ / TQ   Test Figure

TP	ST	TS	PT	QS
a	b	c	d	e

Answer ____

Code Rules:
i) _____
ii) _____

3) AJ / BK / CJ   Test Figure

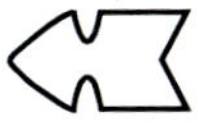

BJ	AK	CK	KB	JC
a	b	c	d	e

Answer ____

Code Rules:
i) _____
ii) _____

4) GR / GS / HR   Test Figure

SG	RD	GH	RS	HS
a	b	c	d	e

Answer ____

Code Rules:
i) _____
ii) _____

5) OW / PX / OY   Test Figure

OX	OP	PY	XP	PW
a	b	c	d	e

Answer ____

Code Rules:
i) _____
ii) _____

© 2012 Stephen Curran

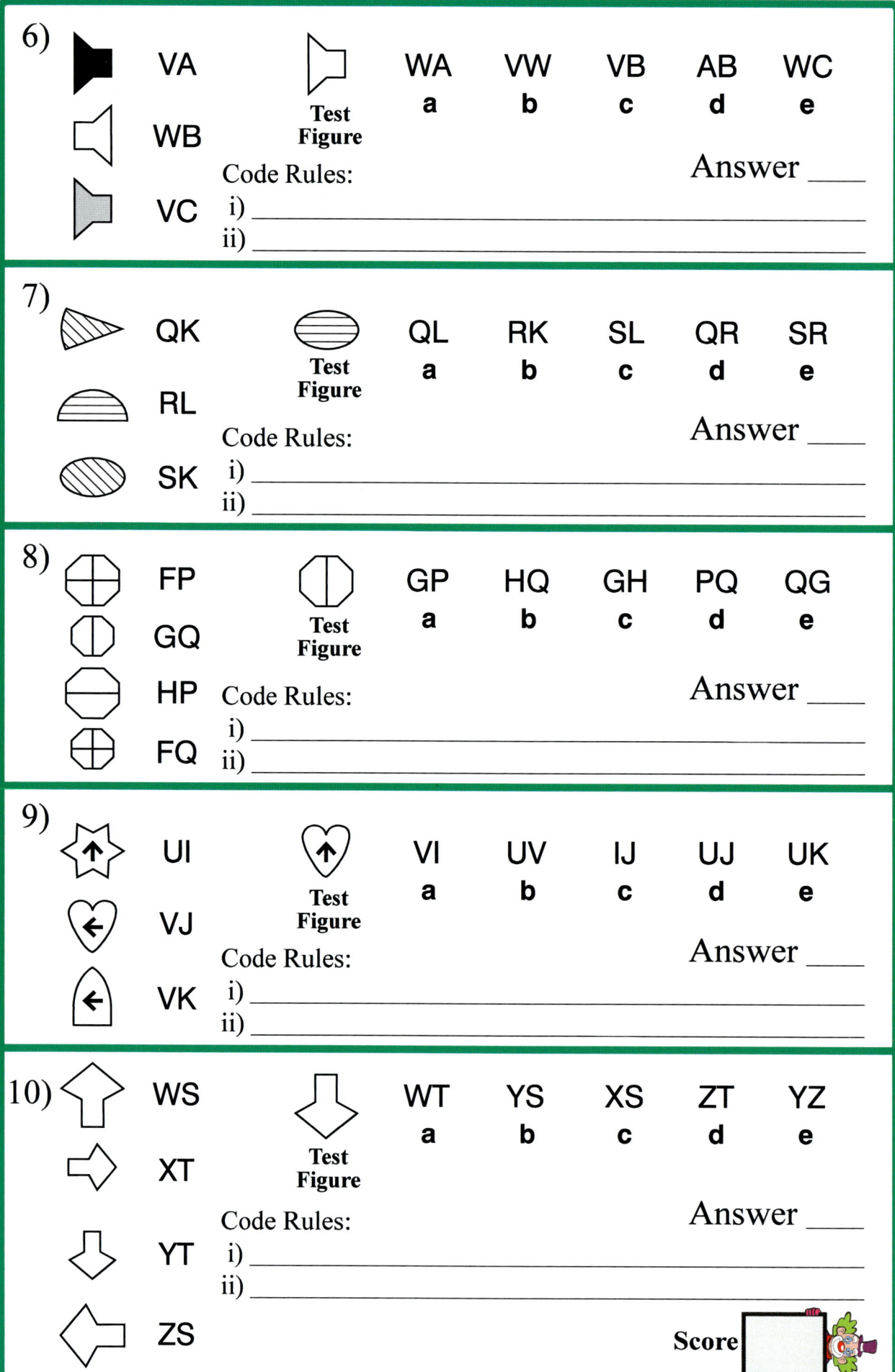

2. Type 2 - Level Two

Type 2 code questions look different but work in the same way as Type 1. This type only ever has two letters, so it always functions as a Level Two question.

Example: Which two letters represent the Test Figure?

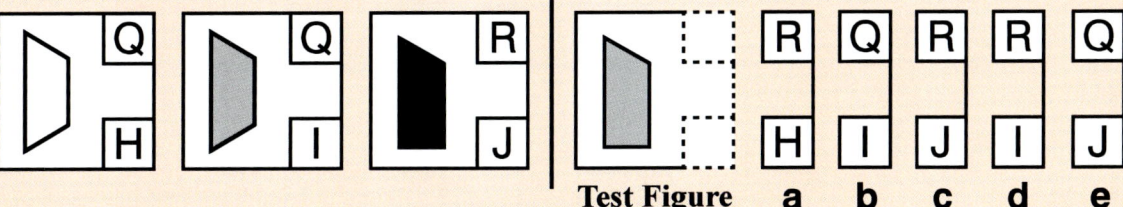

The Code Rules are as follows:

Layer One - Q stands for an Isosceles Trapezium;
R stands for an ordinary Trapezium.
Layer Two - H stands for a White Fill; **I** for a Grey Fill; **J** for a Black Fill.

The Set of Codes:

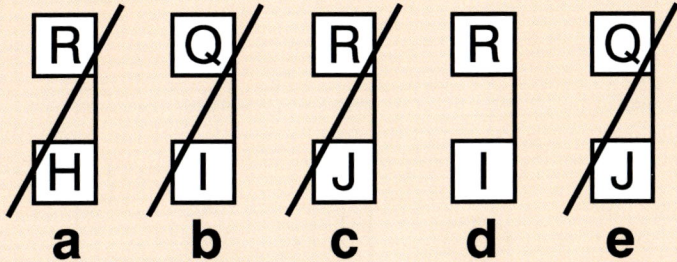

It is important to **eliminate** the wrong possibilities:
b and **e** - QI and QJ are incorrect because they stand for the wrong shape.
a - RH is incorrect because H stands for a White Fill.
c - RJ is incorrect because J stands for a Black Fill.

The Test Figure and the Correct Code:

Layer One
R stands for an ordinary Trapezium.
Layer Two
I stands for a Grey Fill.

Answer: **d - RI** is the correct code.

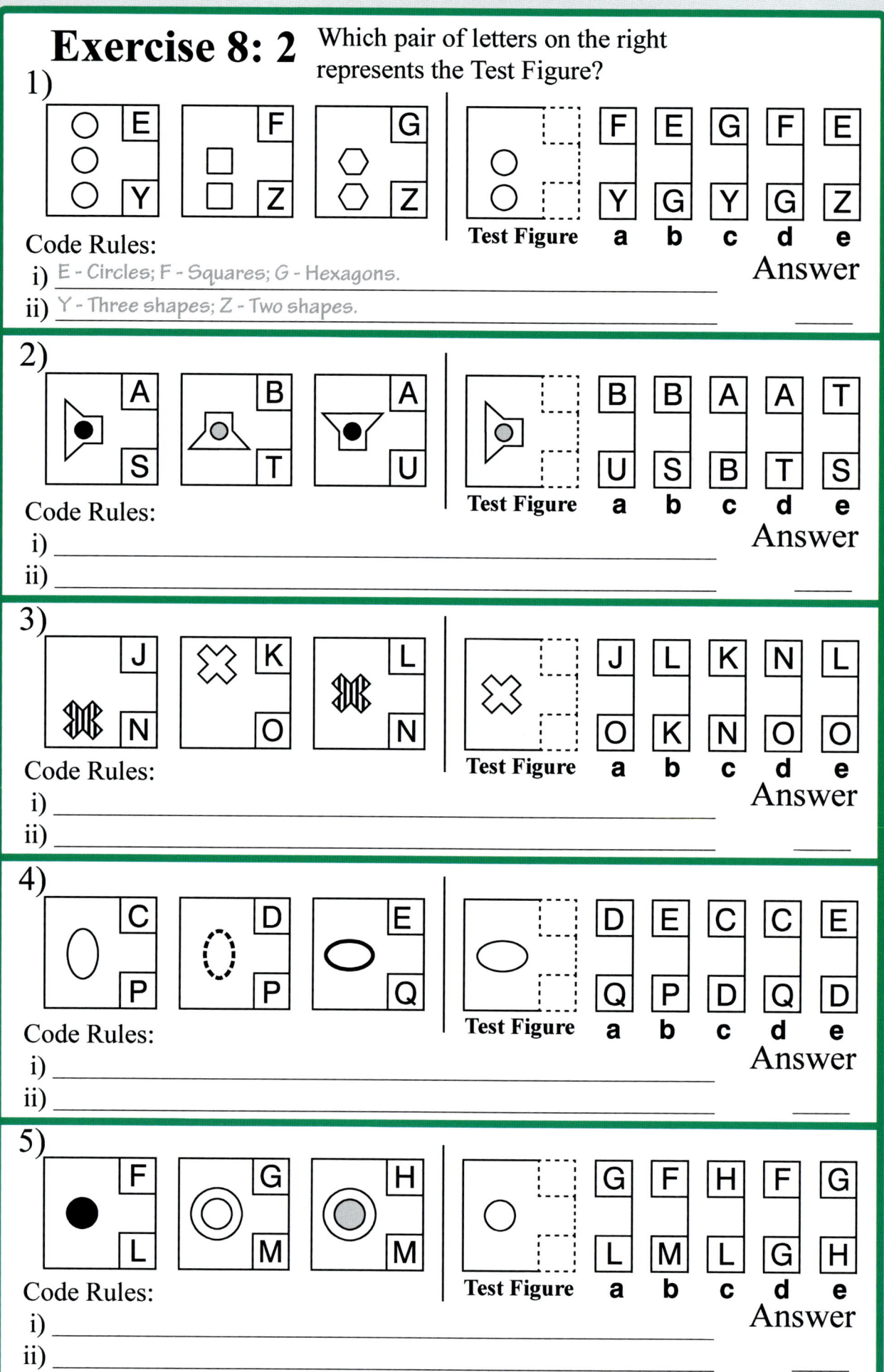

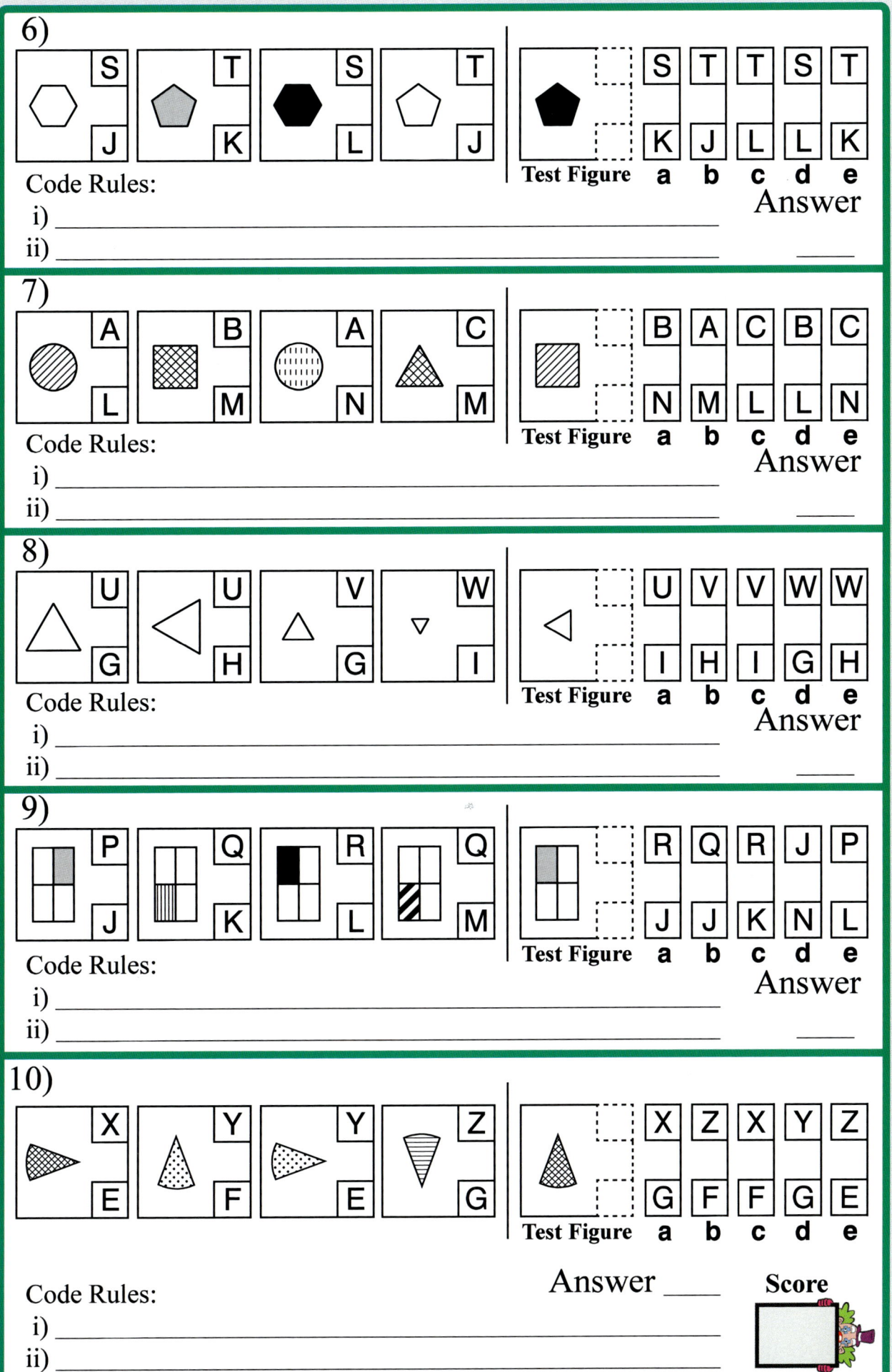

Chapter Nine
ANALOGIES

In Verbal Reasoning, an **Analogy** is a similarity in meaning between two parallel statements or words. This comparison is linked by the word '**as**' which means '**like**'.

For example: **Huge** is to **tiny** as **wide** is to **narrow**

In a Non-verbal Reasoning analogy question, a similarity can be established between two sets of figures.

Example: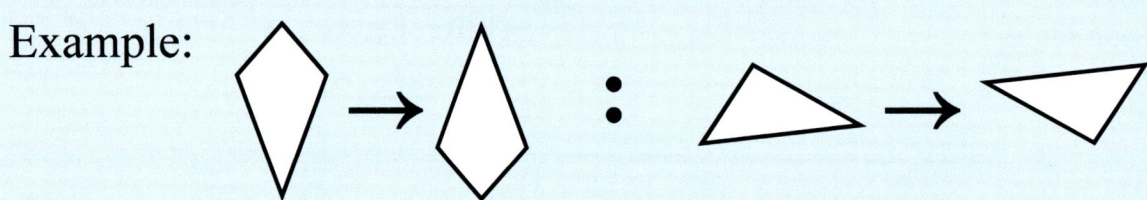

The first Kite rotates 180° to form the second Kite. The **Colon Symbol** (:) in between means '**as**' or '**like**'. Therefore the first Triangle must rotate 180° to form the second Triangle. This now completes the analogy between the two sets of figures.

1. Level One

In a **Level One** analogy question, there is only one layer or change to look for within the first pair of figures. This layer or change will then be applied to the second pair of figures.

Example: Which figure completes the analogy?

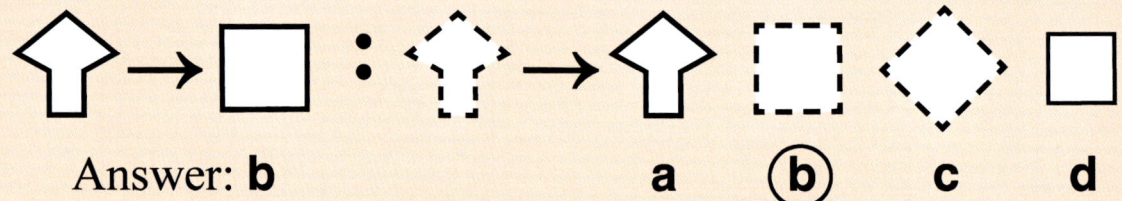

Answer: **b**   a   b   c   d

The Analogy Rule: In the first pair of figures the Arrow with a Solid Line has become a Square with a Solid Line.
The Analogy Rule Applied: In the second pair of figures the Arrow with a Dashed Line has become a Square with a Dashed Line.

Exercise 9: 1 Which figure completes the analogy?

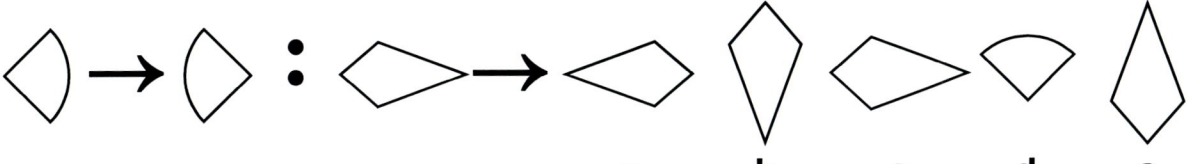

1) Analogy Rule: Answer

The shape has been rotated 180°. _____

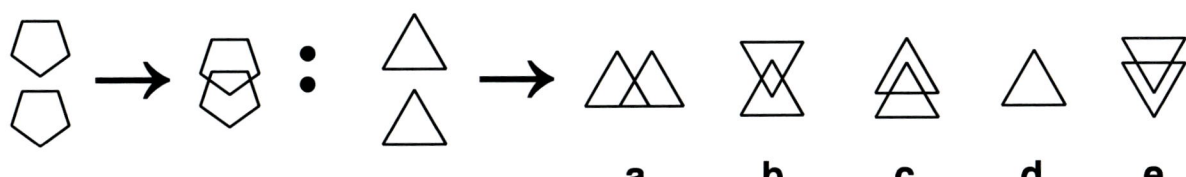

2) Analogy Rule: Answer

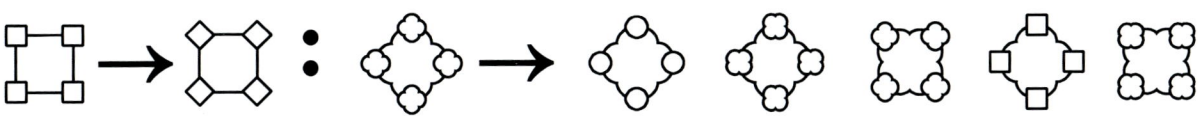

3) Analogy Rule: Answer

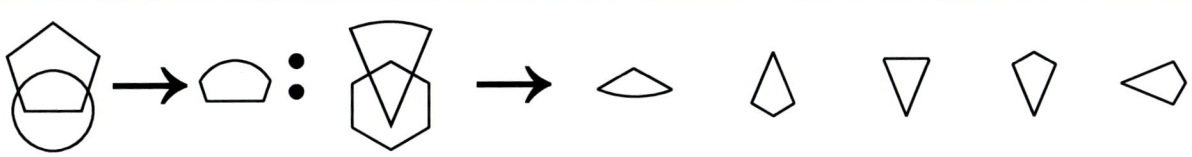

4) Analogy Rule: Answer

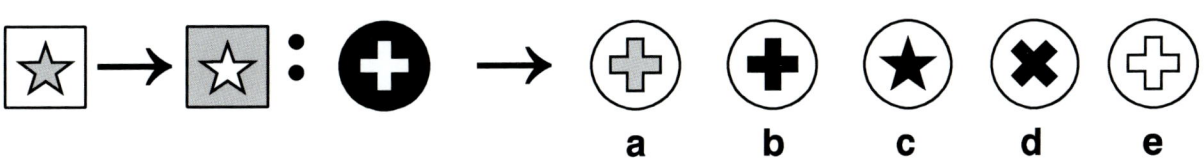

5) Analogy Rule: Answer

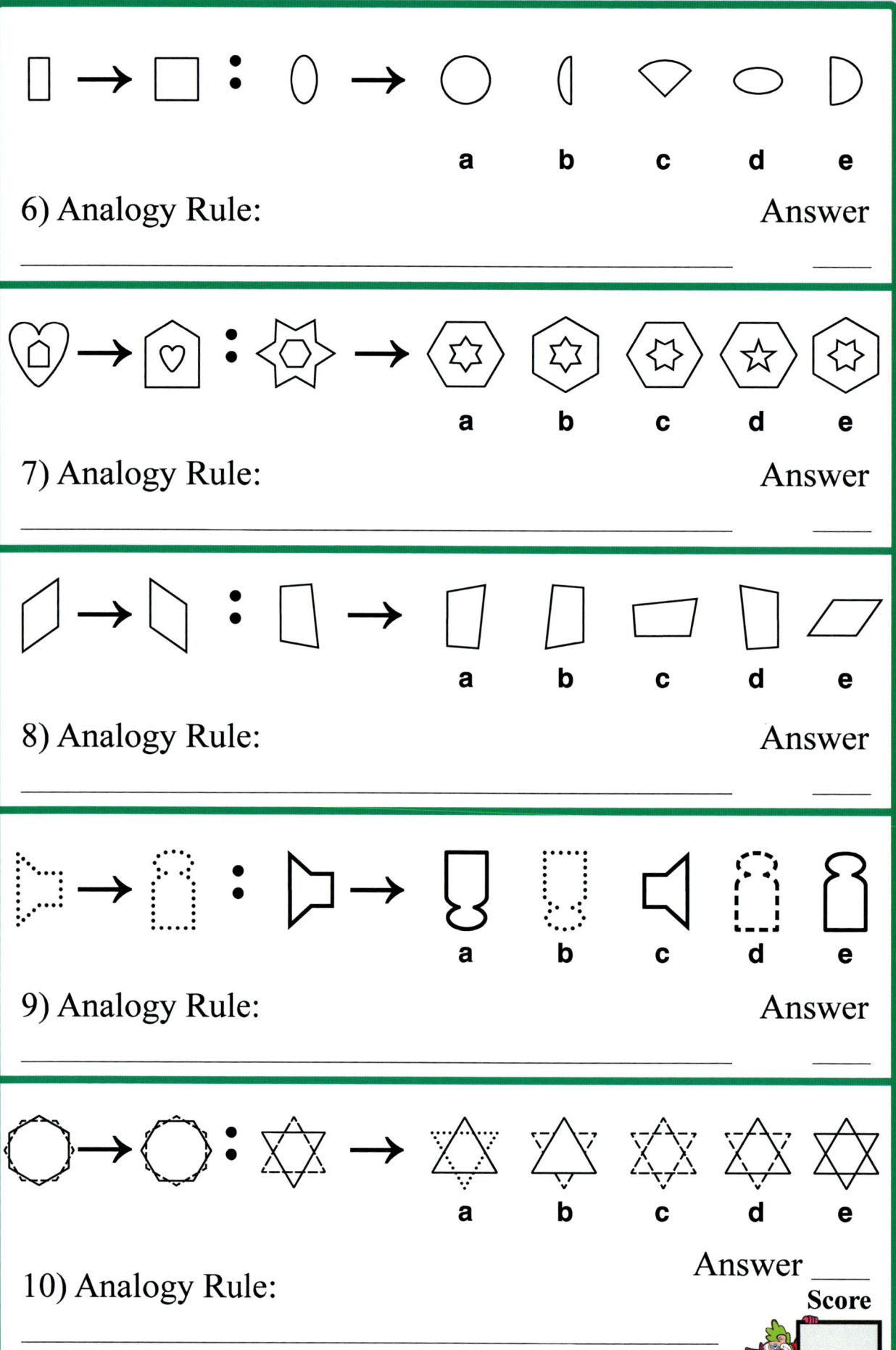

2. Level Two

In **Level Two** analogy questions, there are two layers or changes to look for in the first pair of figures. These layers or changes will then be applied to the second pair of figures.

Example: Which figure completes the analogy?

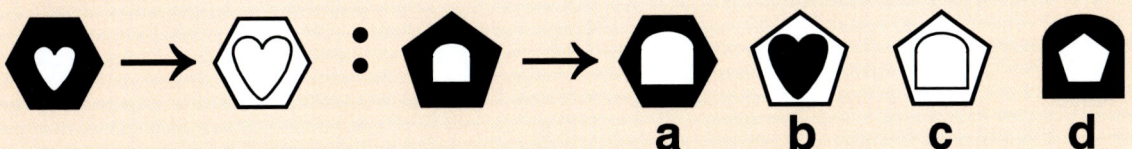

The First Pair of Figures - Analogy Rules:
In the first pair of figures there are two layers or changes:

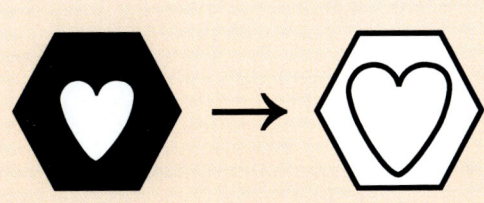

Layer 1 - The Regular Hexagon with a Black Fill has become a Regular Hexagon with a White Fill. There is no change in size.

Layer 2 - The Heart Shape with a White Fill has been enlarged.

The Second Set of Figures:

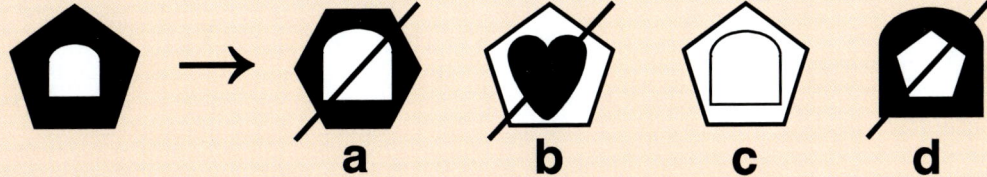

It is important to **eliminate** the wrong possibilities:

a - The Hexagon with a Black Fill should be a Pentagon with a White Fill.

b - The enclosed Heart Shape with a Black Fill should be an enclosed Loaf Shape with a White Fill.

d - The Loaf Shape with a Black Fill should be a Pentagon with a White Fill. The enclosed Pentagon with a White Fill should be an enclosed Loaf Shape with a White Fill.

The Correct Pair of Figures:
In this pairing two correct layers or changes can be identified:

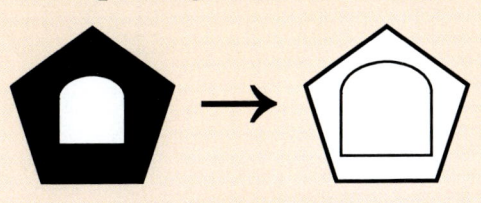

Layer 1 - The Regular Pentagon with a Black Fill has become a Regular Pentagon with a White Fill.

Layer 2 - The Loaf Shape with a White Fill has been enlarged.

Answer: **c**

Exercise 9: 2 Which figure completes the analogy?

1) Analogy Rules:
i) The shape has been rotated 90°.
ii) The same shape with a Grey Fill has been added.

Answer

2) Analogy Rules:
i) _____
ii) _____

Answer

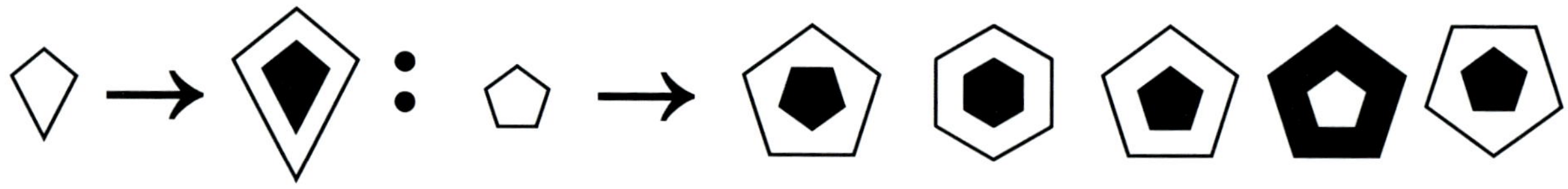

3) Analogy Rules:
i) _____
ii) _____

Answer

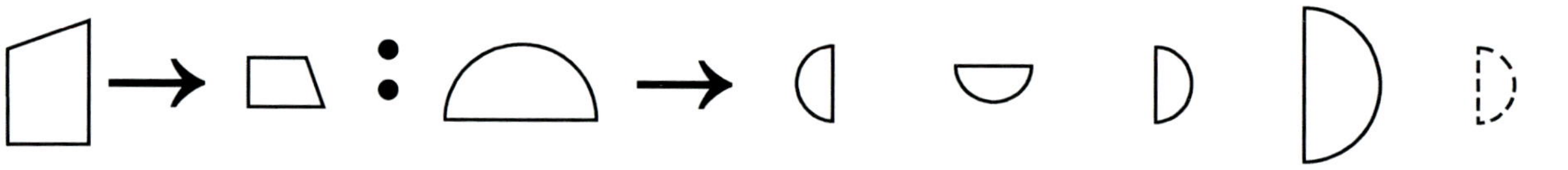

4) Analogy Rules:
i) _____
ii) _____

Answer

5) Analogy Rules:
i) _____
ii) _____

Answer

© 2012 Stephen Curran

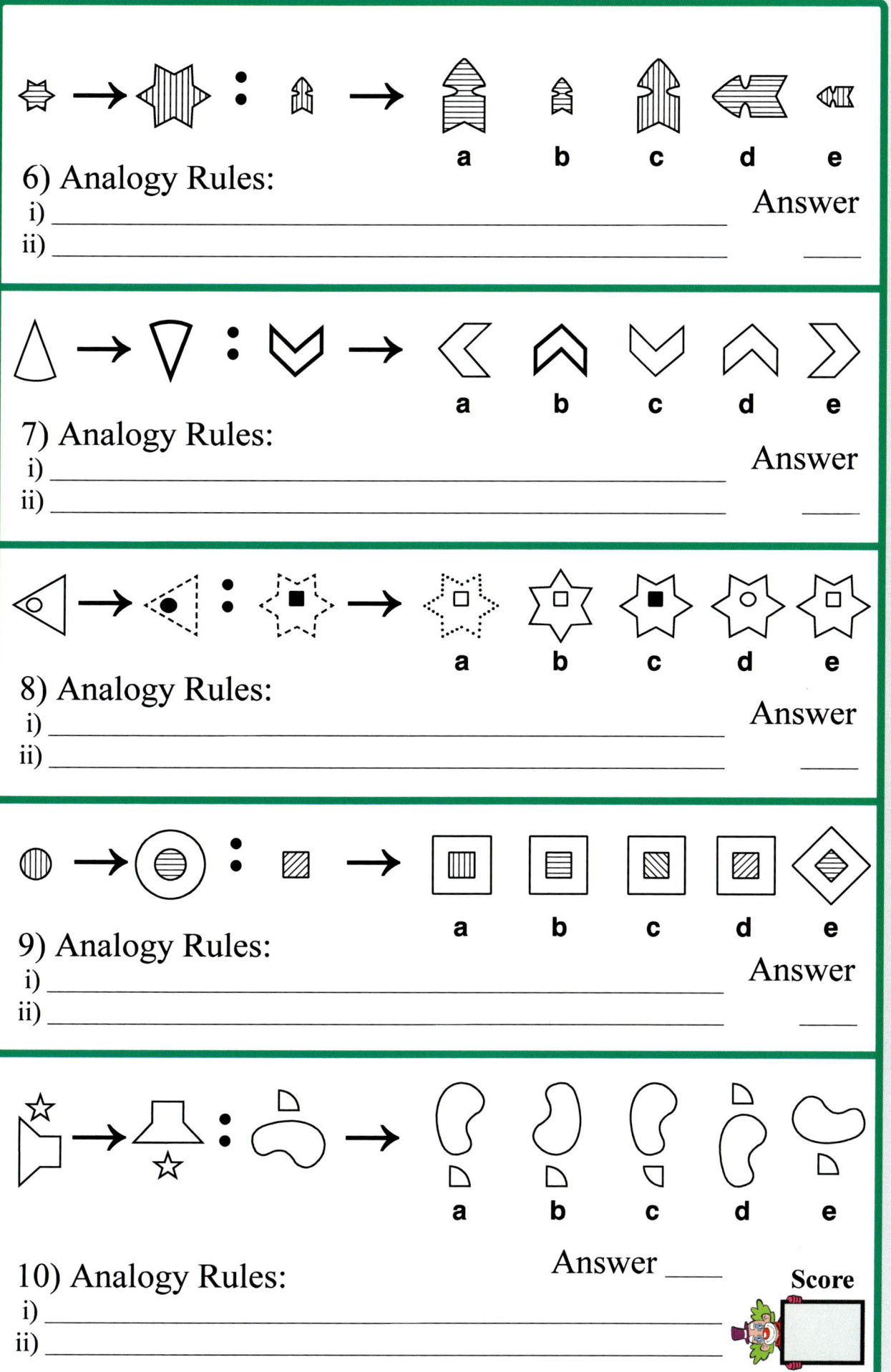

Chapter Ten
SIMILARITIES

In Verbal Reasoning, **Similarity** questions involve selecting two words from two groups that have the closest meaning.

For example: (**conclude   transmit   start**)
              (**organise   begin   associate**)

The two words most similar in meaning are **start** and **begin**. In a Non-verbal Reasoning similarity question, a strong likeness can be established between two or more shapes.

Example:

The two Shield Shapes are most similar as they belong to the same family of shapes.

1. Level One

In **Level One** similarity questions, there is only one layer or similarity to look for between the figures.

Example: Which figure on the right is most like the two figures on the left?

                                  a   **b**   **c**   **ⓓ**   **e**

Answer: **d**

The Similarity Rule that connects the figures on the left is: A small Square with a Black Fill must be enclosed within the larger shape. This is only true for figure **d**.

Note: A similarity rule only counts if it helps select the correct alternative by eliminating the wrong ones. In the above example, all the figures have an enclosed shape with a Black Fill. As they all share this similarity, it does not count as a similarity rule.

Exercise 10: 1

Which figure on the right is most similar to those on the left?

1)

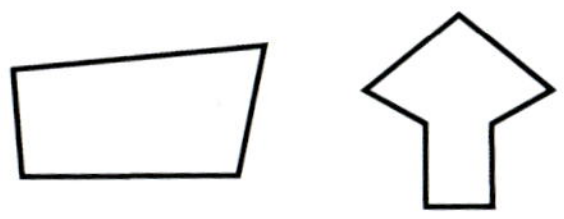

Answer ___

a b c d e

Similarity Rule: _The shape is Straight-edged._

2)

Answer ___

a b c d e

Similarity Rule: _____

3)

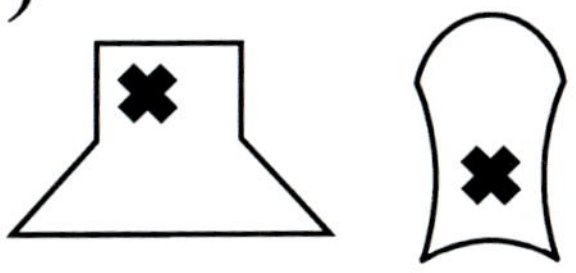

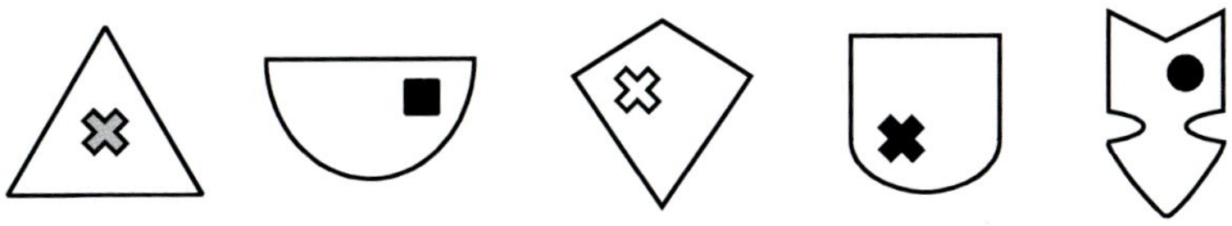

Answer ___

a b c d e

Similarity Rule: _____

4)

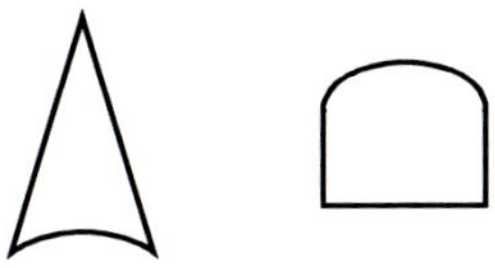

Answer ___

a b c d e

Similarity Rule: _____

5)

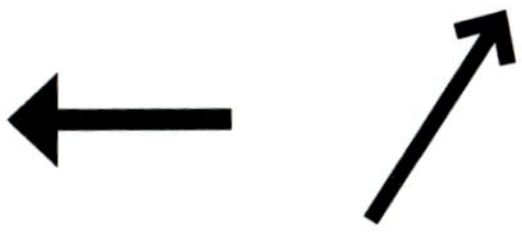

Answer ___

a b c d e

Similarity Rule: _____

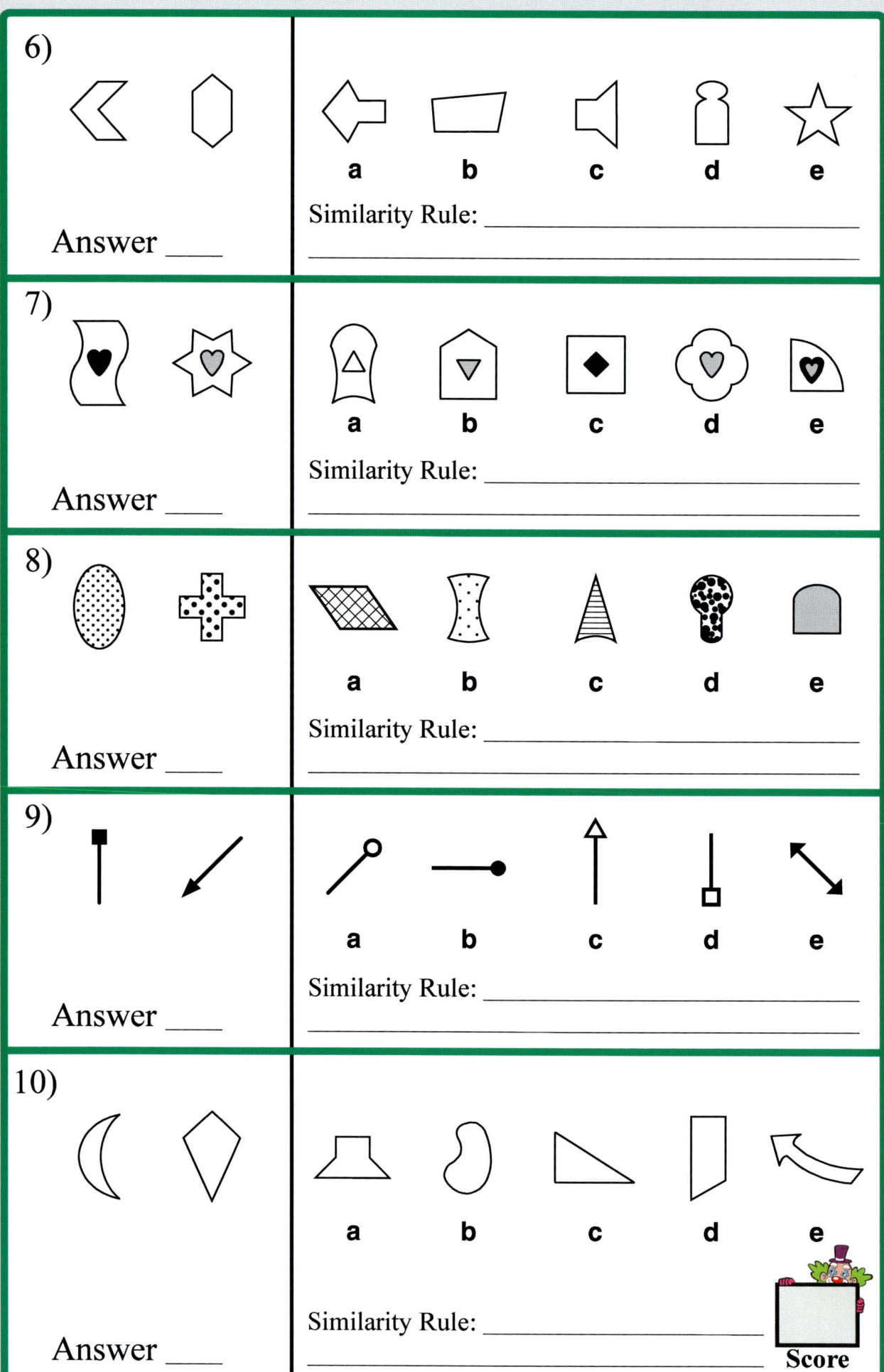

2. Level Two

In **Level Two** similarity questions, there are two layers or similarities to look for between the figures.

Example: | Which figure on the right is most like the two figures on the left? |

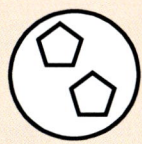 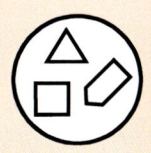   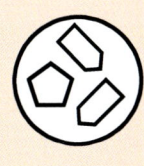 

                                          a   **b**   **c**   **d**

The Rules of Similarity:

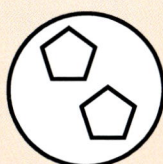    **Layer 1** - The shapes are either identical or completely different.
Layer 2 - The shapes are either in groups of two or three.

Remember: The rules are only relevant if they help to select the right alternative and eliminate the wrong ones.

The Set of Figures:

    a   **b**   **c**   **d**

It is important to **eliminate** the wrong possibilities:
a - There are two identical shapes and one shape is different.
b - There should be no more than three shapes.
c - There are two identical shapes and one shape is different.

The Correct Figure:

   This figure follows the rules of similarity.
Layer 1 - All the Triangles are identical.
Layer 2 - The Triangles are in a group of three.
Answer: **d**

Exercise 10: 2

Which figure on the right is most similar to those on the left?

1)

a b c d e

Similarity Rules → i) The outer shape has a Dotted Line.
Answer ____   ii) The enclosed shape has a Thick Solid Line.

2)

a b c d e

Similarity Rules → i) _____
Answer ____   ii) _____

3)

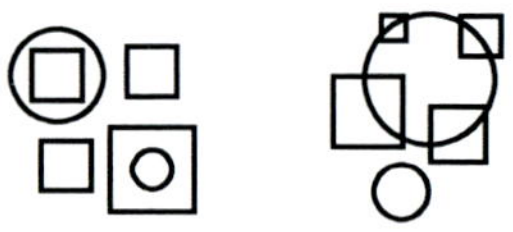

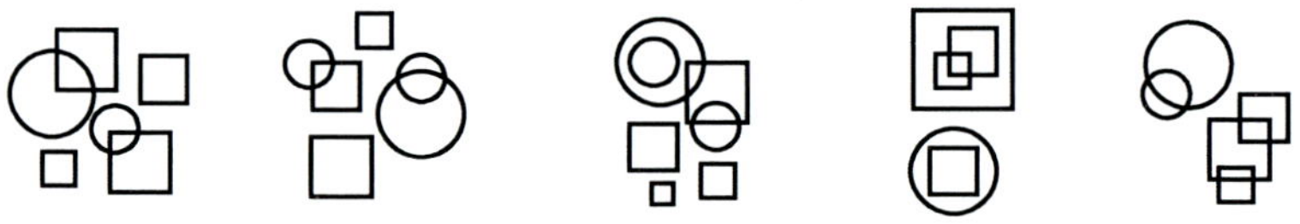

a b c d e

Similarity Rules → i) _____
Answer ____   ii) _____

4)

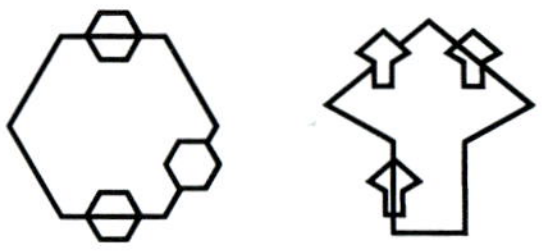

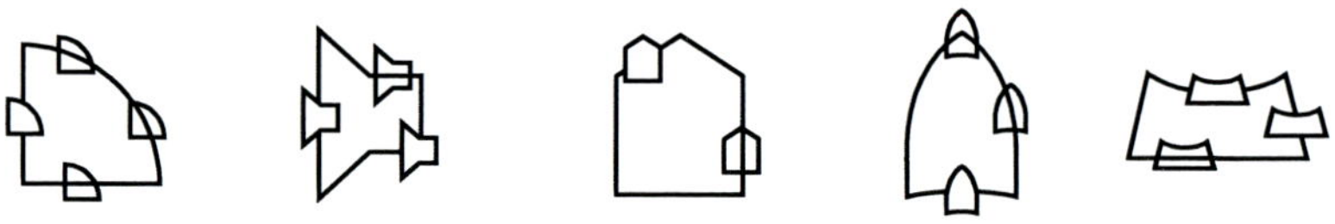

a b c d e

Similarity Rules → i) _____
Answer ____   ii) _____

5)

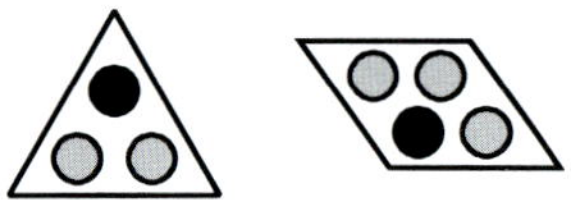

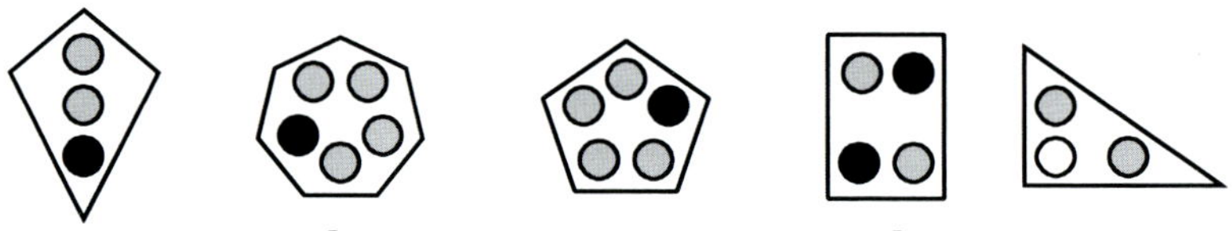

a b c d e

Similarity Rules → i) _____
Answer ____   ii) _____

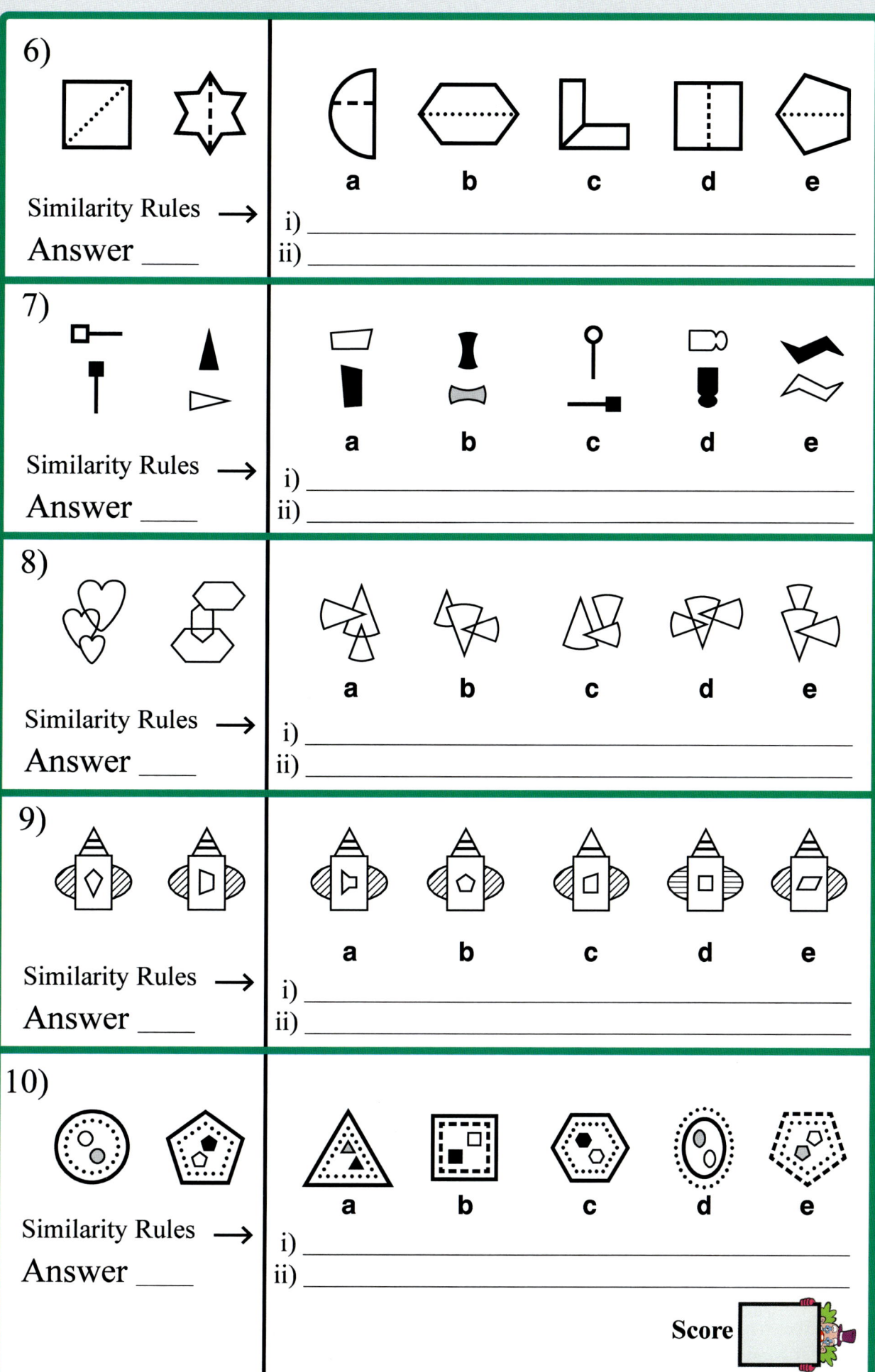

Chapter Eleven
SERIES

Series questions in Verbal Reasoning can be either:
Letter Sequences or **Number Sequences**
Letter or number patterns can be **Repetitive** or **Cumulative**.
Repetitive - One letter is missing each time.

For example: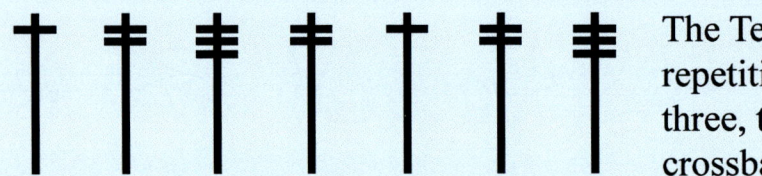

Cumulative - The gap between the numbers gets larger.

For example: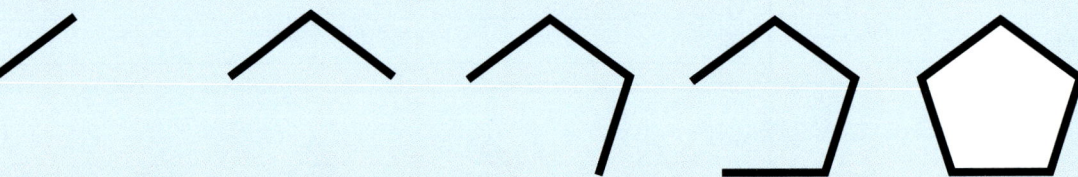

Series questions in Non-verbal Reasoning are of two types:
Shapes can be arranged in a repetitive pattern:

The Telegraph Poles are in a repetitive pattern of one, two, three, two, one, two, three crossbars, etc.

Shapes can be be arranged in a Cumulative Pattern:

The Pentagon builds side by side in five stages.

1. Level One

In **Level One** series questions, there is only one layer or change to look for between the figures.

Example: Which figure is missing in the series?

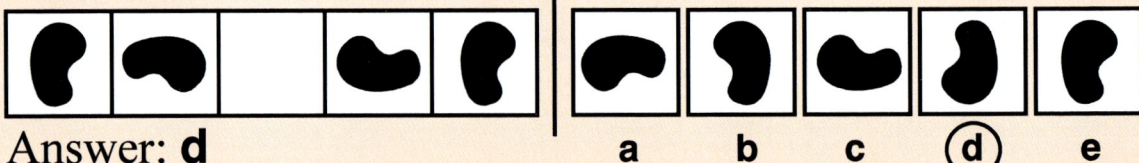

Answer: **d**

The Bean Shape is rotated 90° clockwise each time.

Note: In series questions, a rule only occurs if it indicates something that changes as the series progresses, e.g. it is not necessary to say the shape is always a Bean.

Exercise 11: 1

Which figure on the right completes the series on the left?

1) Answer ____

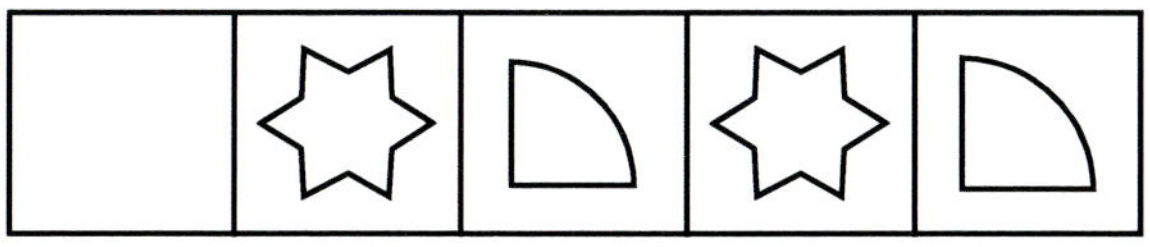

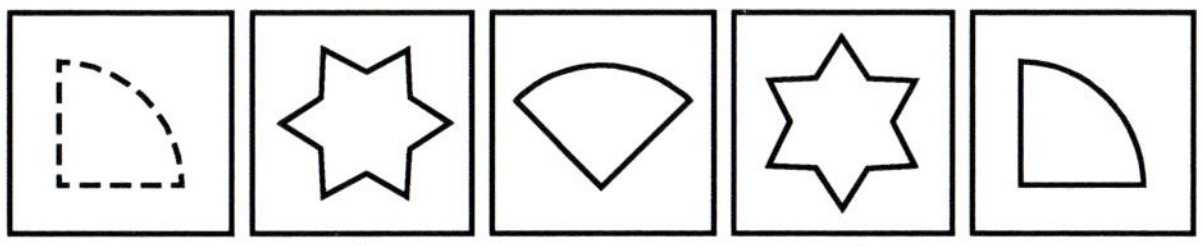

a b c d e

Series Rule:

The Quadrant and Star alternate at each stage.

Repetitive or Cumulative?

Repetitive.

2) Answer ____

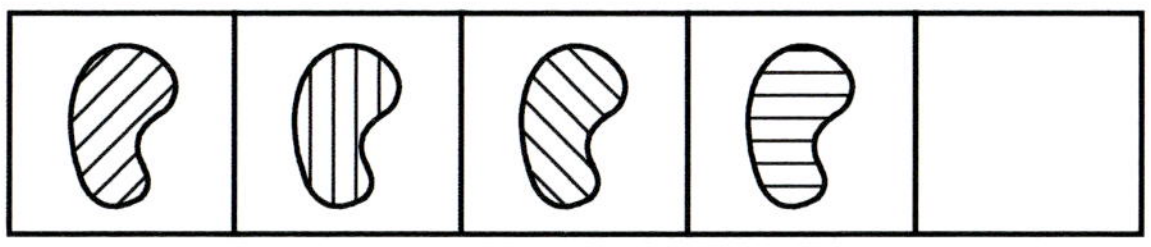

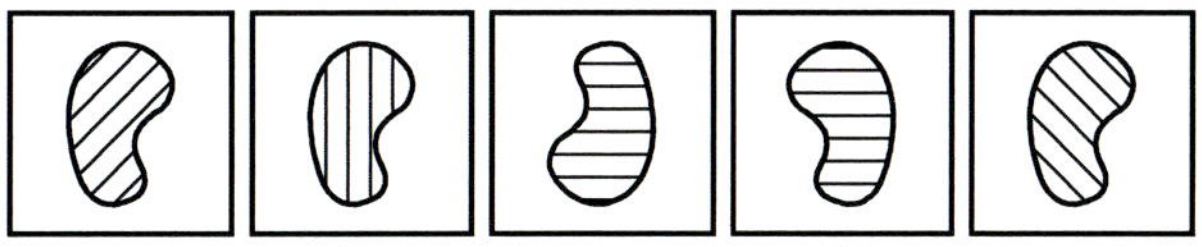

a b c d e

Series Rule:

____

____

Repetitive or Cumulative?

____

3) Answer ____

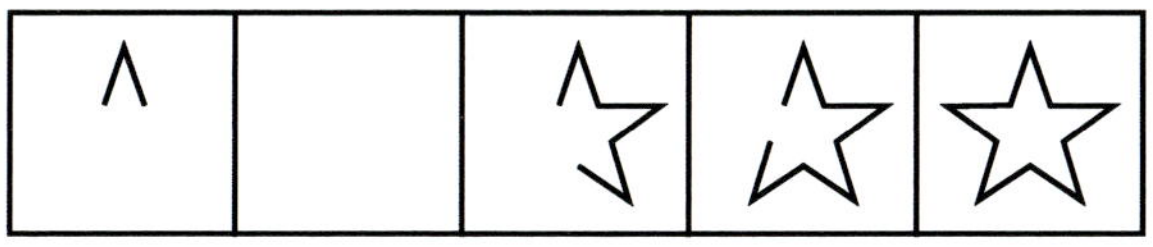

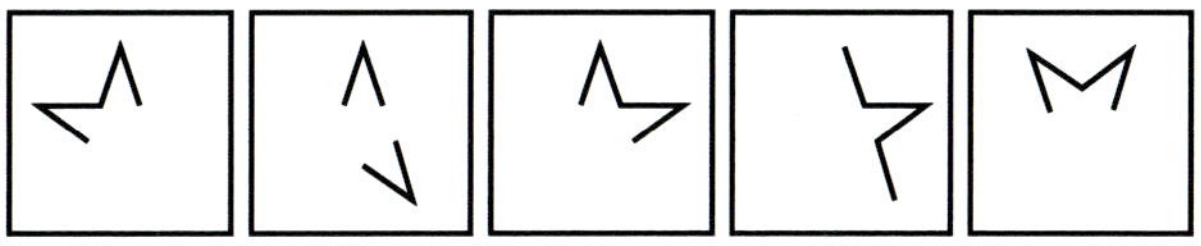

a b c d e

Series Rule:

____

____

Repetitive or Cumulative?

____

4) Answer ____

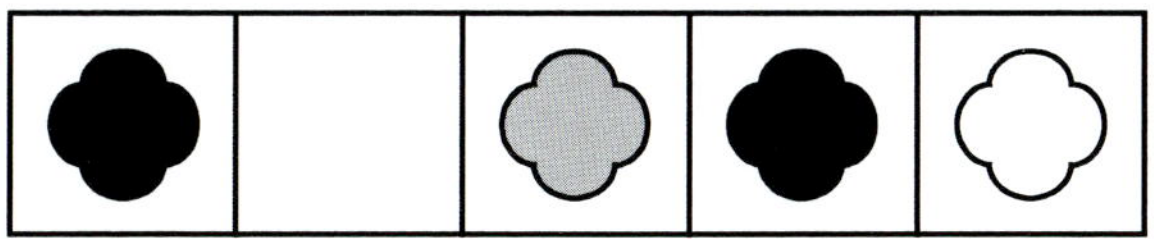

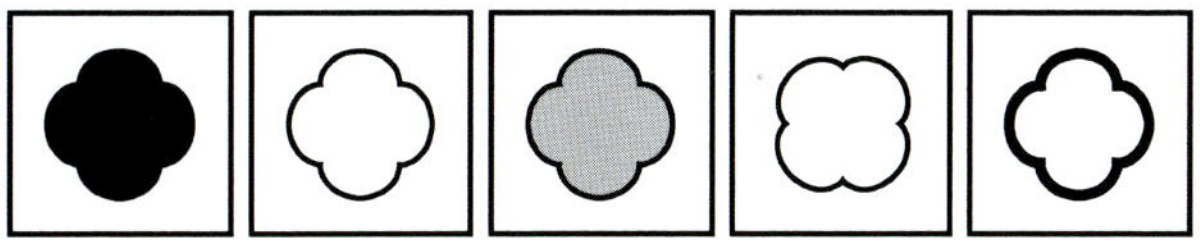

a b c d e

Series Rule:

____

____

Repetitive or Cumulative?

____

5) Answer ____

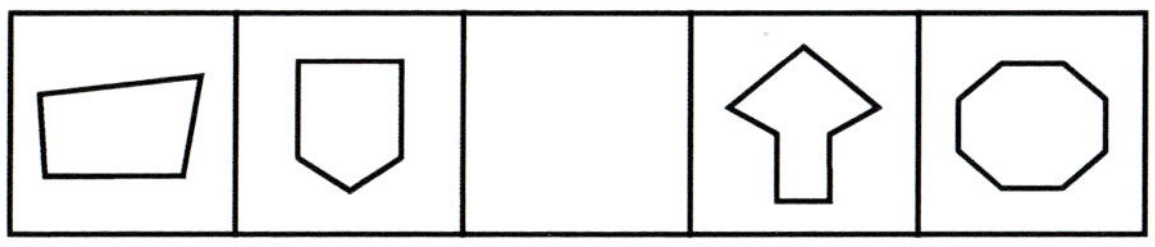

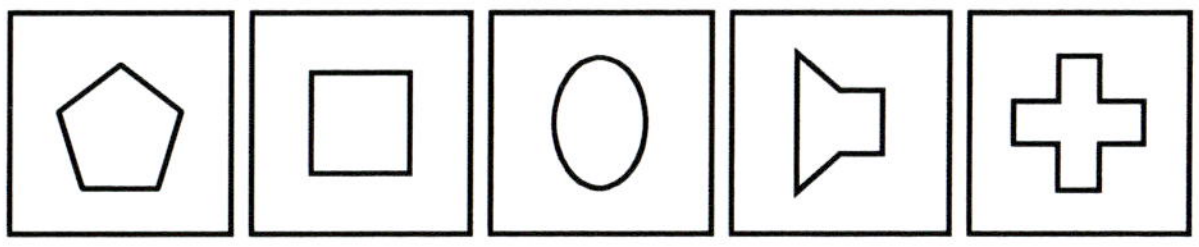

a b c d e

Series Rule:

____

____

Repetitive or Cumulative?

____

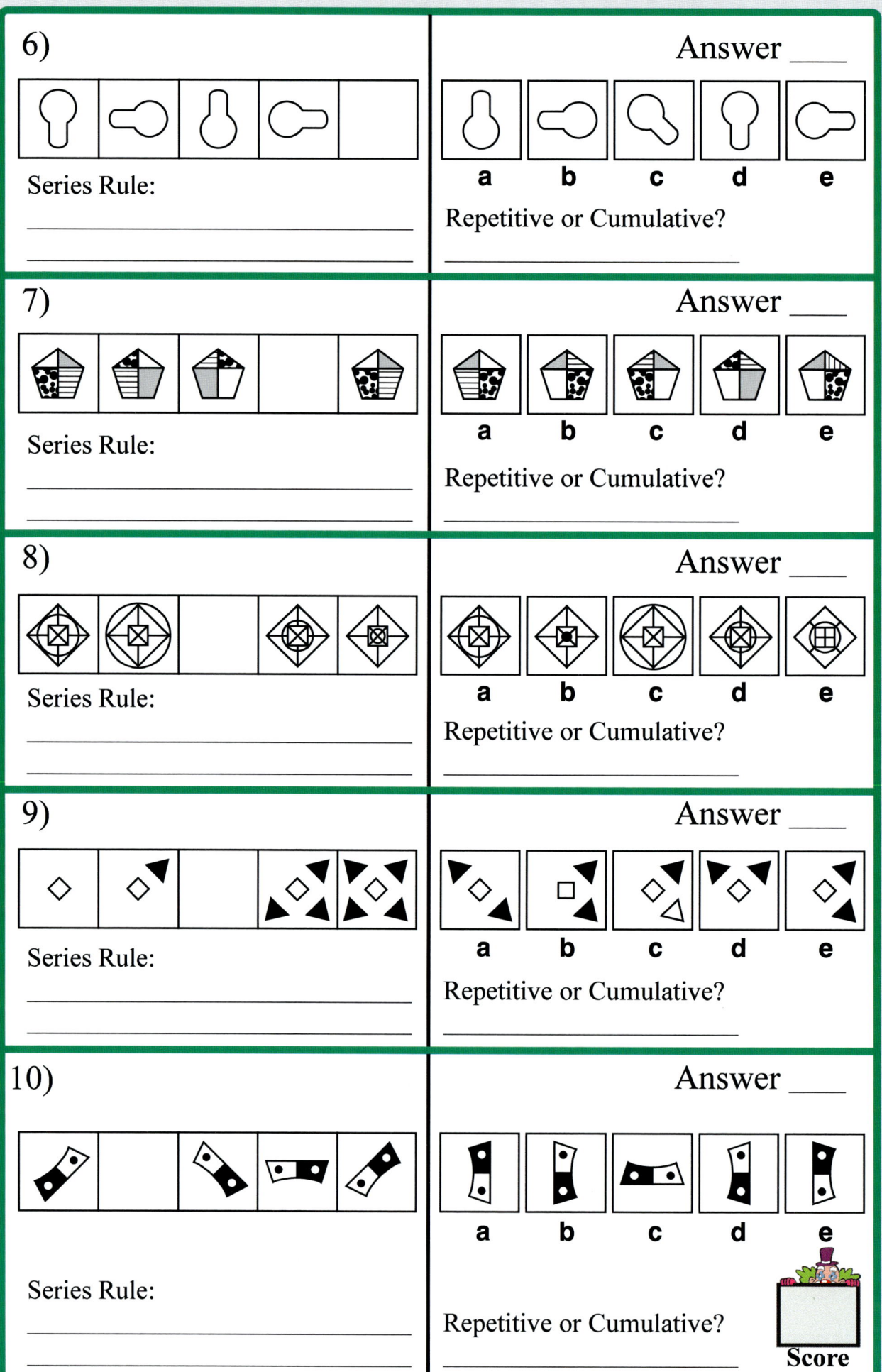

2. Level Two

In **Level Two** series questions, there are two layers or changes to look for in the sequence of figures.

Example: Which figure is missing in the series?

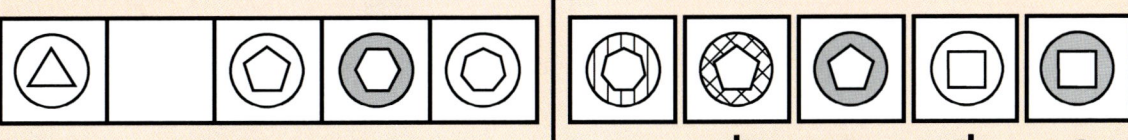

The Series Rules:

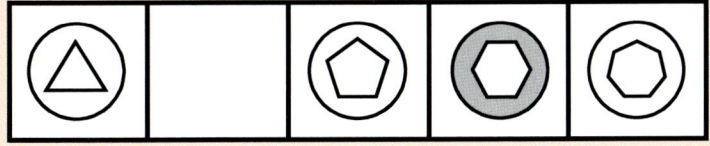

Layer 1 - The fills in the Circle alternate between White and Grey (repetitive).
Layer 2 - The frequency (number) of sides of the enclosed shape increases by one each stage (cumulative).

Remember: In series questions, a rule only occurs if it indicates something that changes as the series progresses, e.g. it is not necessary to say the outer shape is always a Circle.

The Set of Figures:

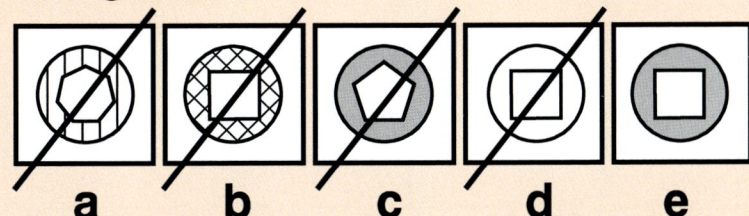

It is important to **eliminate** the wrong possibilities:
a - The Circle has a Shaded Fill and the enclosed shape is a Heptagon.
b - The Circle has a Cross-hatched Lattice Fill.
c - The enclosed shape is a Pentagon.
d - The Circle has a White Fill.

The Correct Figure:

This figure follows the series rules.
Layer 1 - The fill in the Circle should be Grey (repetitive).
Layer 2 - The enclosed shape should have four sides (cumulative).

Answer: **e**

Exercise 11: 2

Which figure on the right completes the series on the left?

1) Answer ____

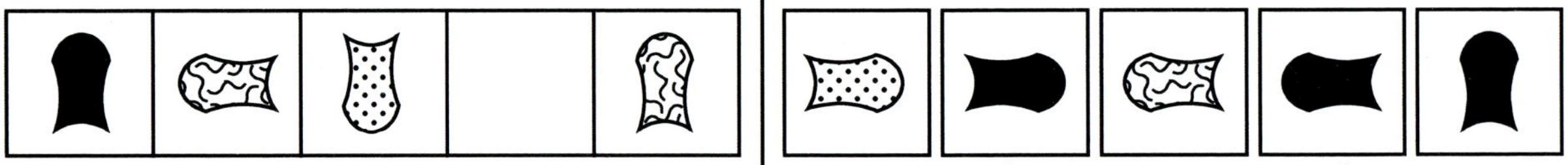

a b c d e

Series Rules:

i) The shape rotates 90° anticlockwise.

ii) The fills alternate Solid, Liquid, Dotted, etc. at each stage.

2) Answer ____

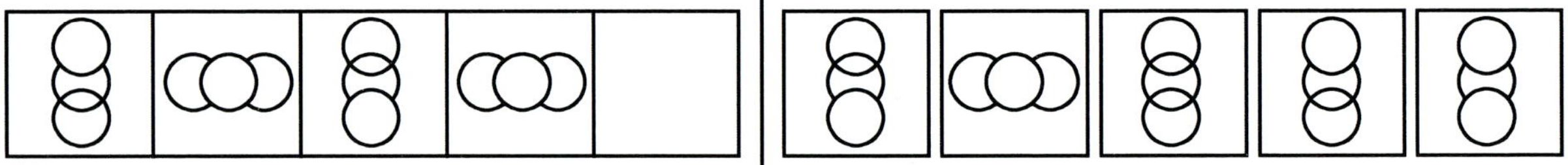

a b c d e

Series Rules:

i) ______________________________

ii) ______________________________

3) Answer ____

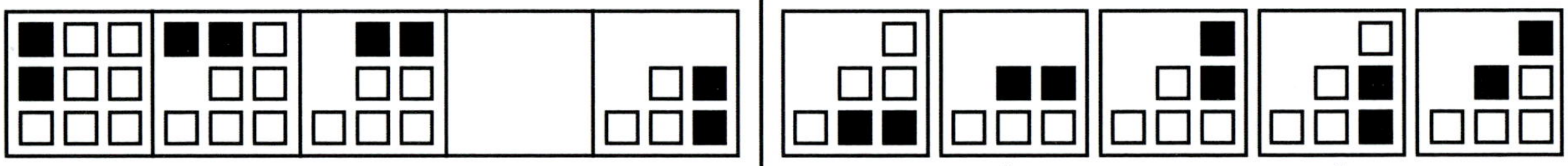

a b c d e

Series Rules:

i) ______________________________

ii) ______________________________

4) Answer ____

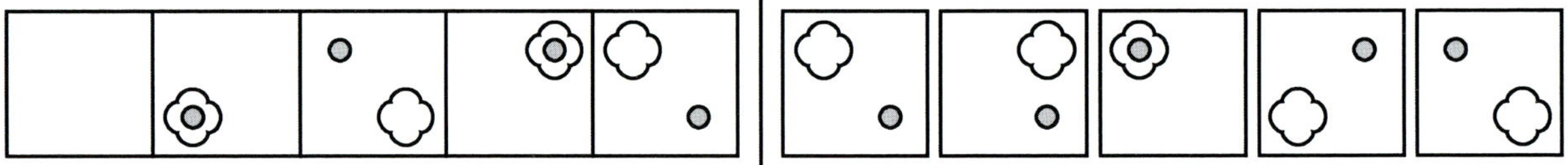

a b c d e

Series Rules:

i) ______________________________

ii) ______________________________

5) Answer ____

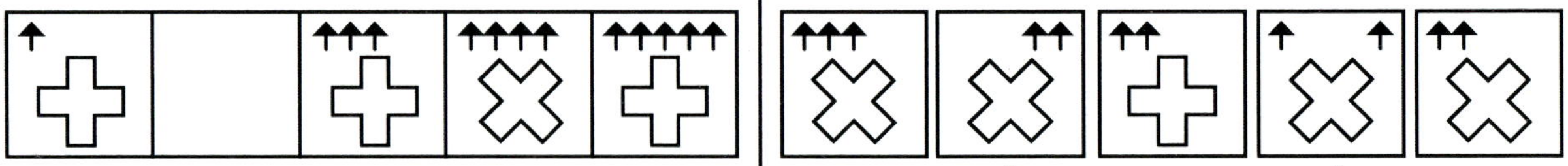

a b c d e

Series Rules:

i) ______________________________

ii) ______________________________

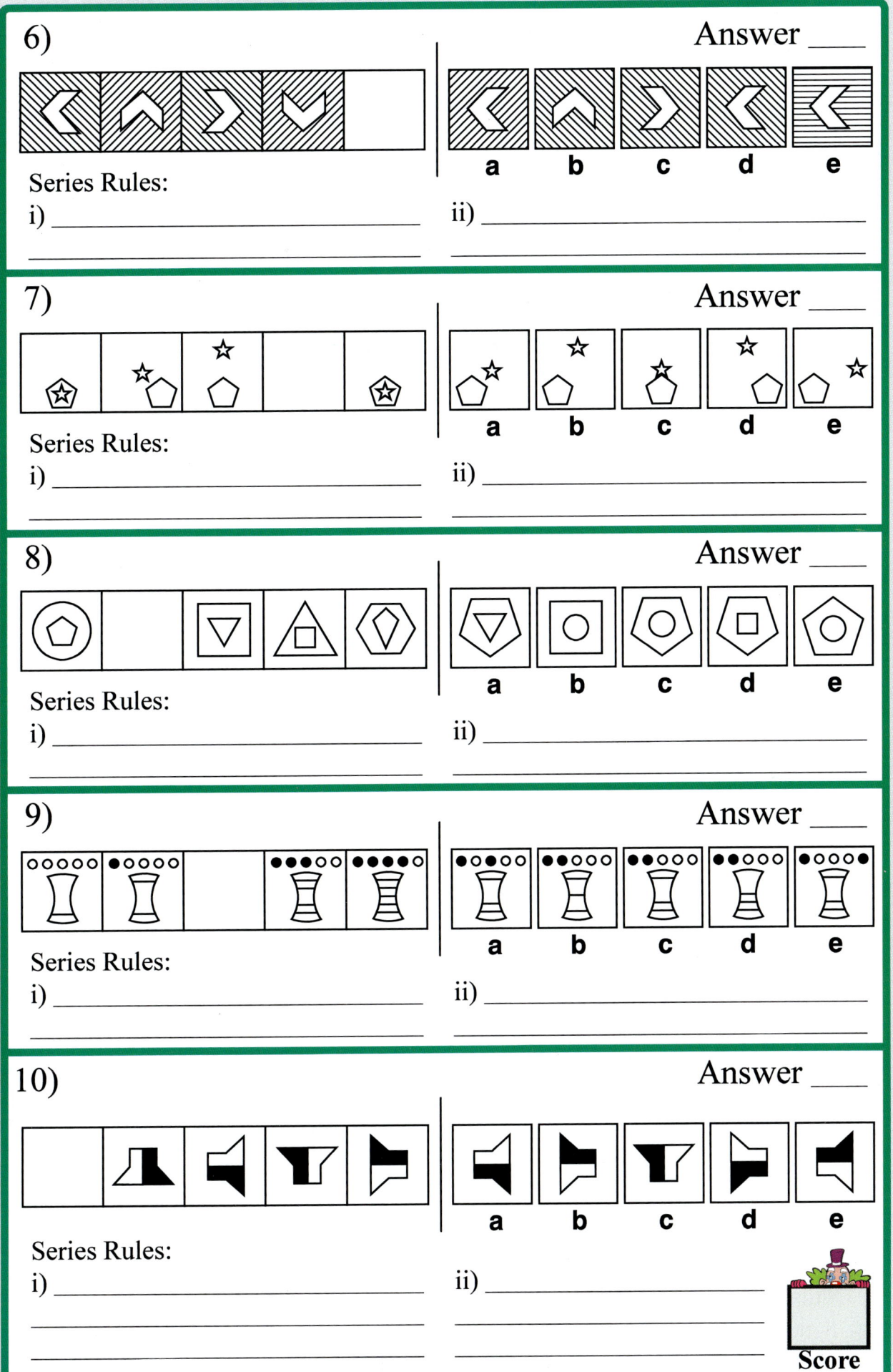

Chapter Twelve
MATRICES

Matrices occur in mathematics rather than Verbal Reasoning.

For example: This matrix adds up to **30** in every direction: horizontally, vertically and diagonally.

12	7	11
9	10	11
9	13	8

Matrices are able to test all the key Non-verbal Reasoning skills needed to identify:

Similarity • **Difference** • **Pattern**

A matrix can combine these other question types:

Odd One Out • Analogy • Similarity • Series

1. Level One

In **Level One** matrix questions, there is only one layer or change to look for. Matrix questions are of two types:

1) A Four Square Matrix.

Example: Which figure should fill the empty square?

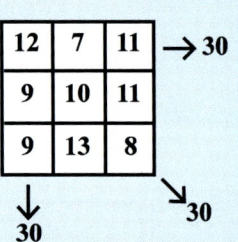     

ⓐ b c d e

Answer: **a**

Four Square Matrices are **analogies** and can work horizontally, vertically and diagonally. This matrix analogy works both horizontally and vertically.

Horizontal - Triangle with a White Fill to Triangle with a Black Fill.
- Square with a White Fill to Square with a Black Fill.

Vertical - Triangle with a White Fill to Square with a White Fill.
- Triangle with a Black Fill to Square with a Black Fill.

2) A Nine Square Matrix.

Example: Which figure should fill the empty square?

  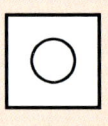   

a b c ⓓ e

Answer: **d**

This Nine Square Matrix works as a **series** or **pattern**.

Each column and row must have all three shapes: Heart Shape, Churn Shape, Circle. The Circles with Shaded Fills lie along a right slant diagonal line.

Exercise 12: 1

Which figure on the right completes the matrix on the left?

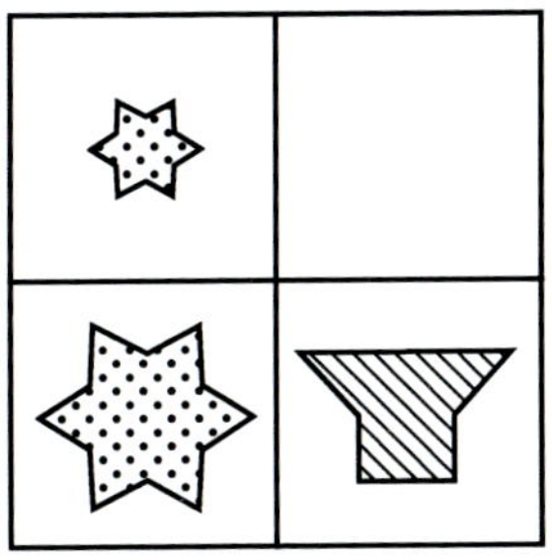

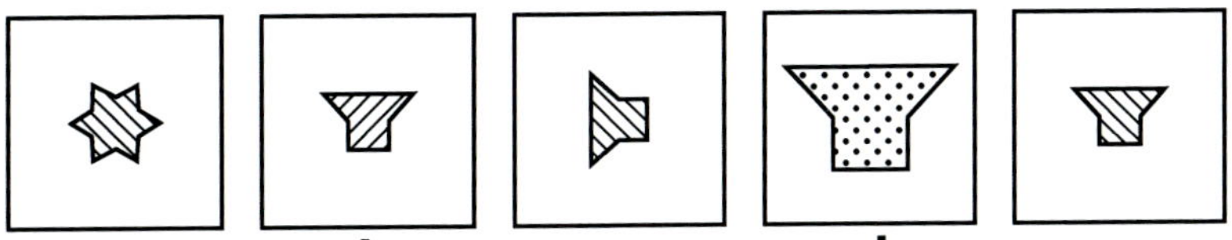

a b c d e

1) Matrix Rule: This matrix is best solved vertically .

The shape reduces and keeps its fill.

Answer ____

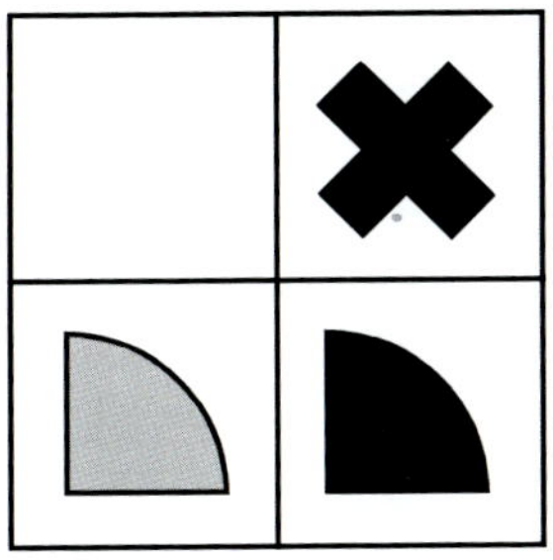

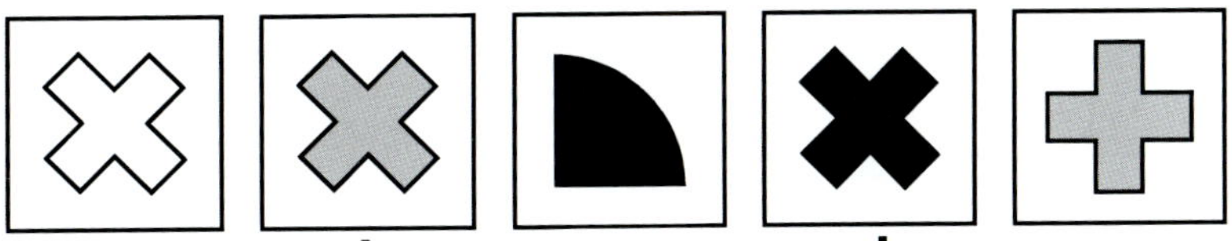

a b c d e

2) Matrix Rule: This matrix is best solved __________ .

Answer ____

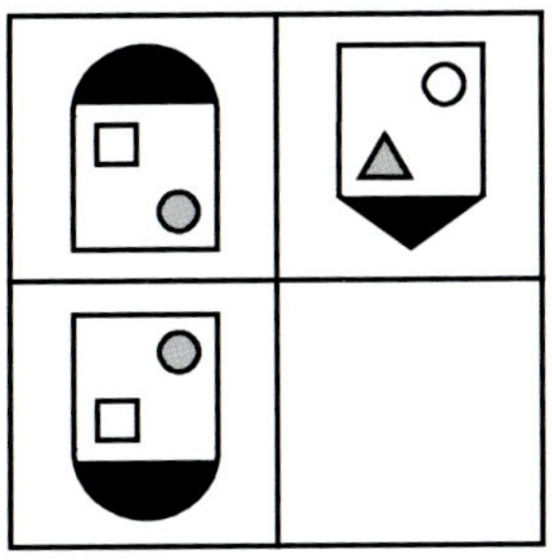

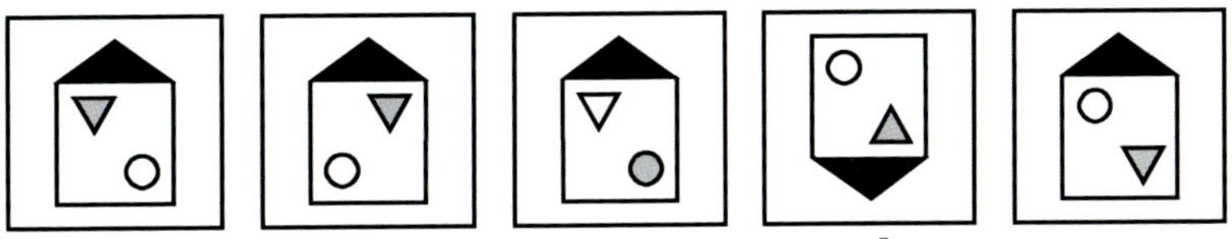

a b c d e

3) Matrix Rule: This matrix is best solved __________ .

Answer ____

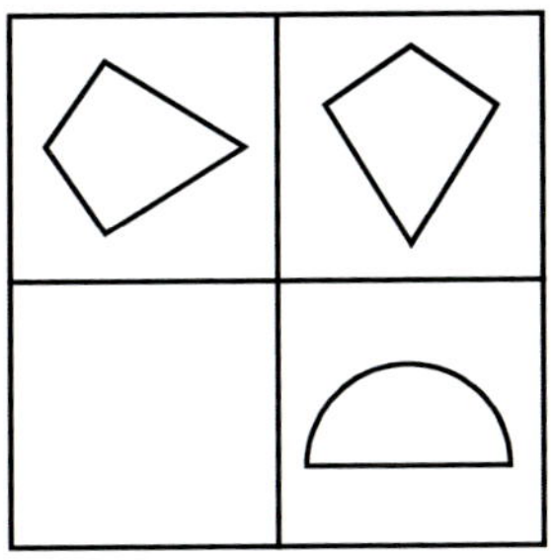

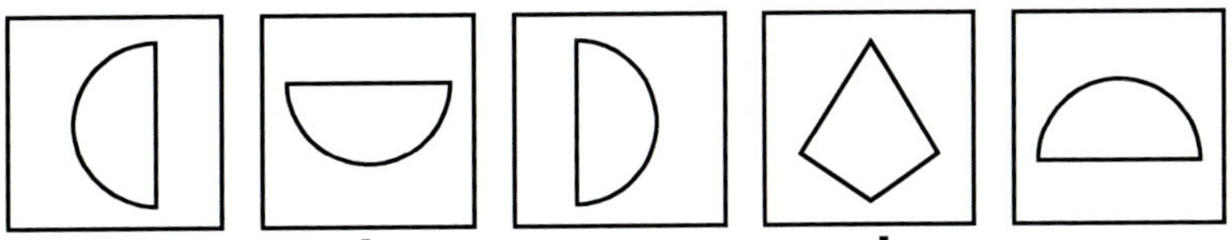

a b c d e

4) Matrix Rule: This matrix is best solved __________ .

Answer ____

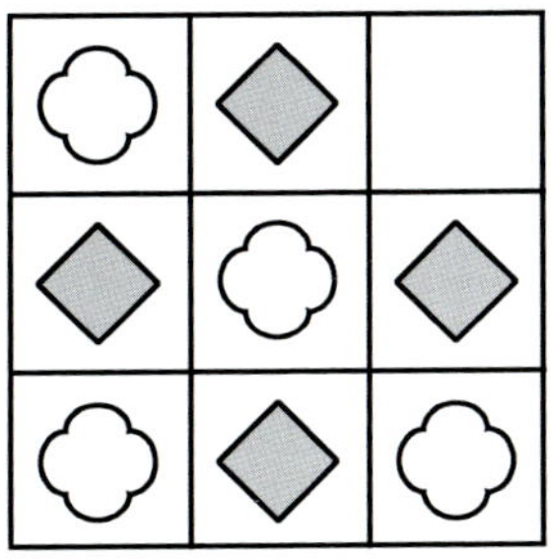

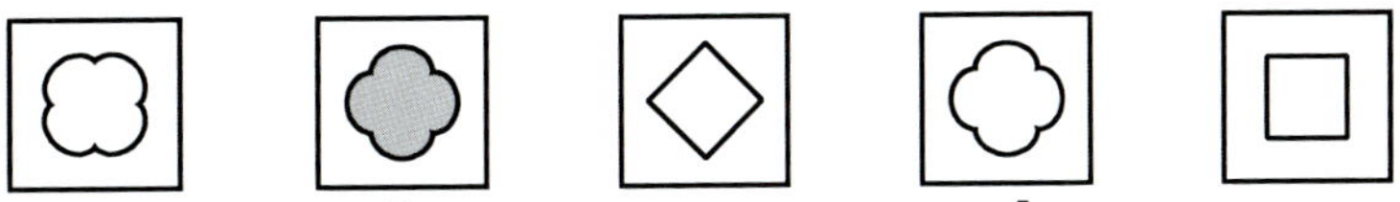

a b c d e

5) Matrix Rule: This matrix is best solved __________ .

Answer ____

Answer ____

a b c d e

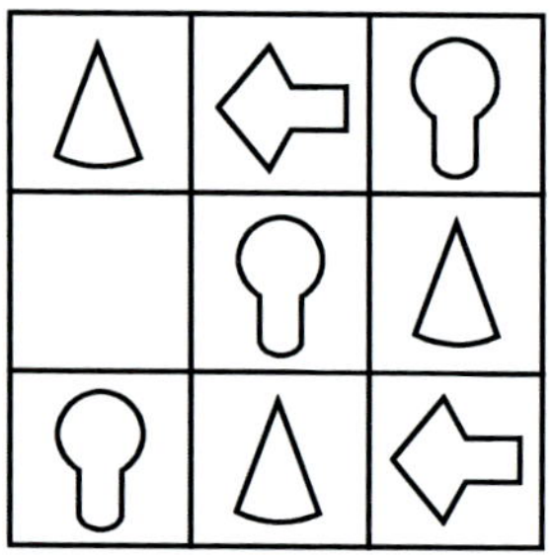

6) Matrix Rule: This matrix is best solved ____________.

____

____

Answer ____

a b c d e

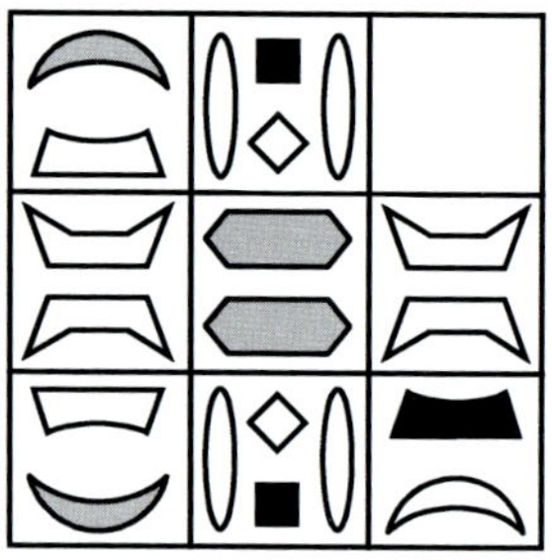

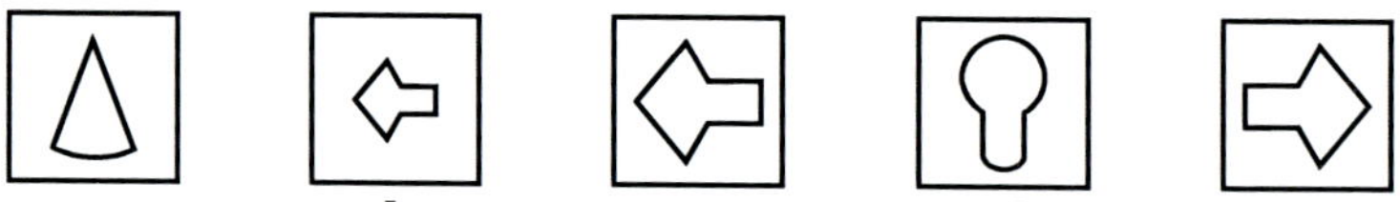

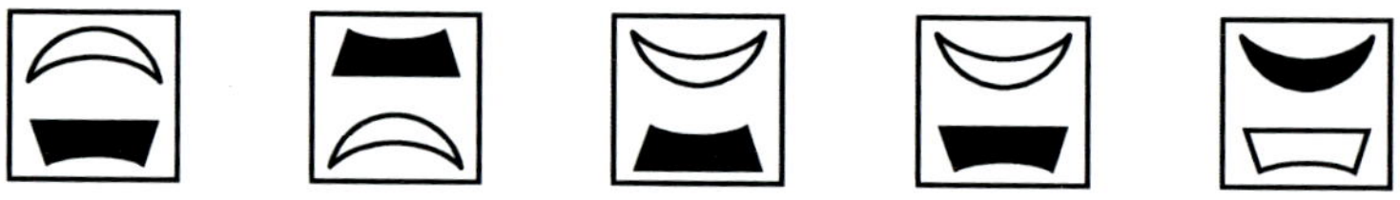

7) Matrix Rule: This matrix is best solved ____________.

____

____

Answer ____

a b c d e

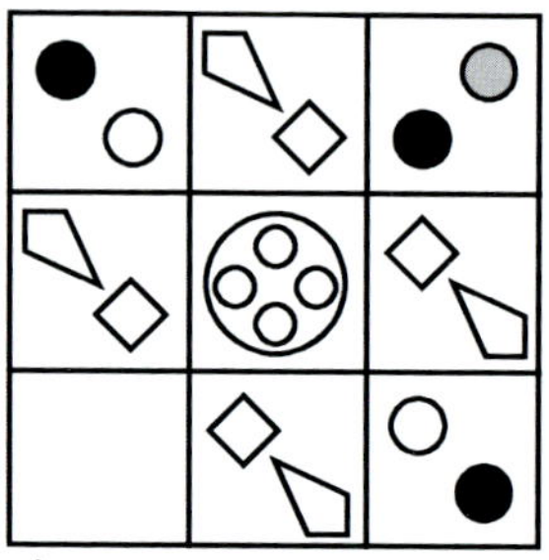

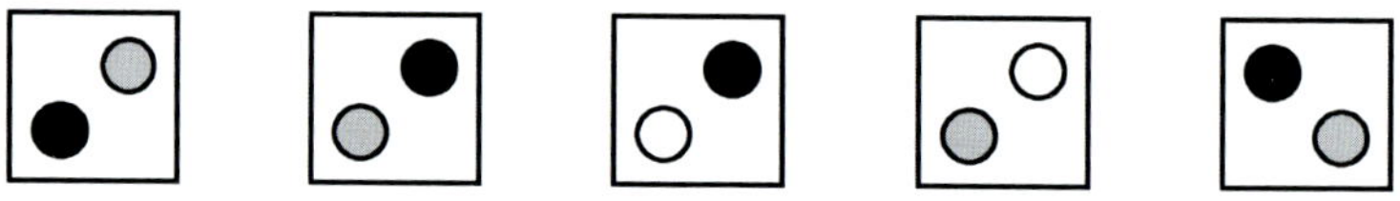

8) Matrix Rule: This matrix is best solved ____________.

____

____

Answer ____

a b c d e

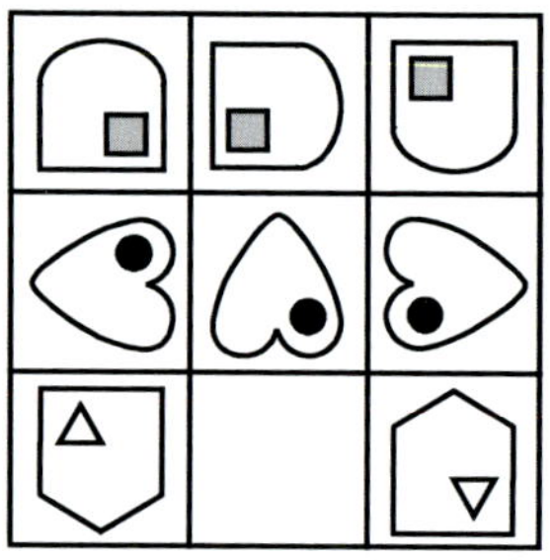

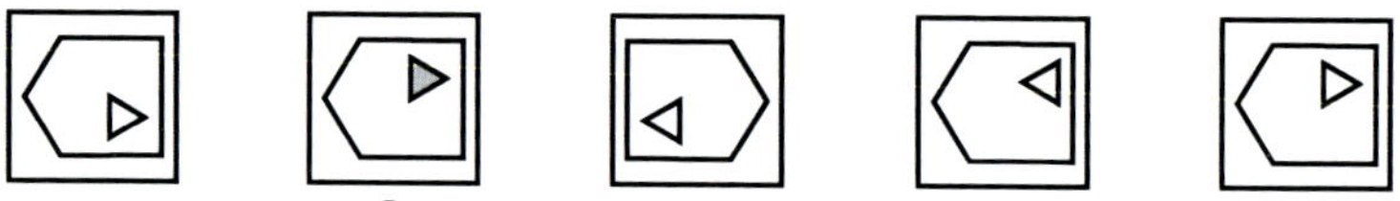

9) Matrix Rule: This matrix is best solved ____________.

____

____

Answer ____

a b c d e

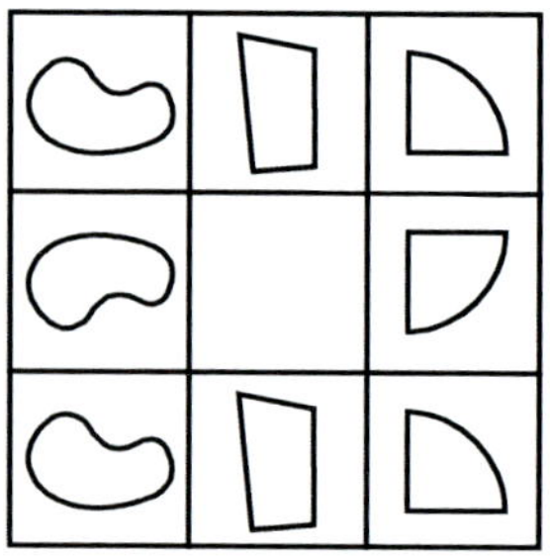

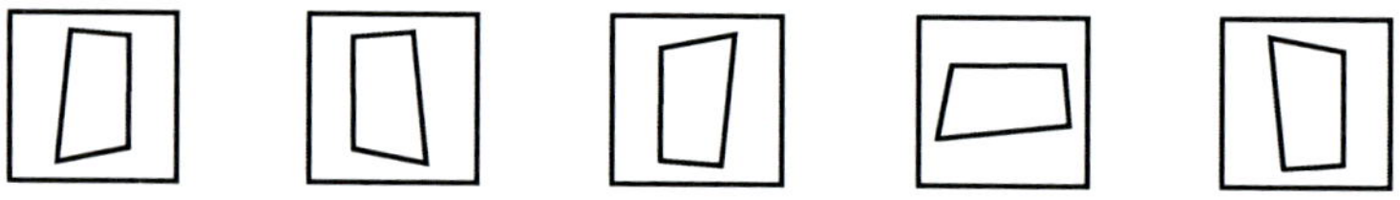

10) Matrix Rule:
This matrix is best solved ____________.

____

____

Score

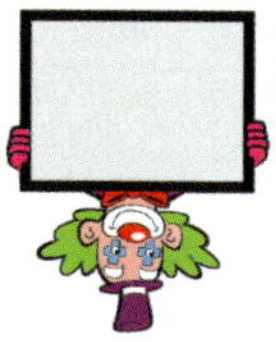

2. Level Two

In **Level Two** matrix questions, there are two layers or changes to look for between the shapes or figures.

Example: Which figure should fill the empty square?

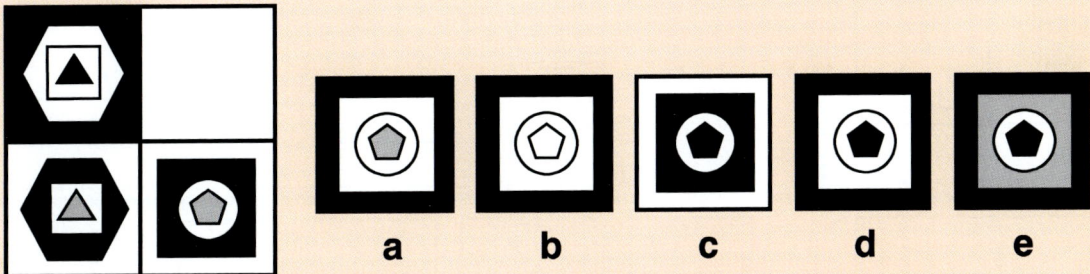

The Matrix Rules:

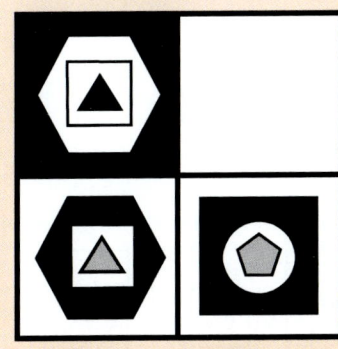

This matrix analogy works horizontally and vertically (by row and by column). However these rules are best established vertically (upwards) as the shapes are of the same type.

Layer 1 - The fills of the outer two shapes reverse: Black goes to White, White goes to Black.

Layer 2 - The Grey Fill in the smallest enclosed shape becomes Black.

Note: If the shapes in either a row or column are of the same type, it is best to establish the rules in that direction.

The Set of Figures:

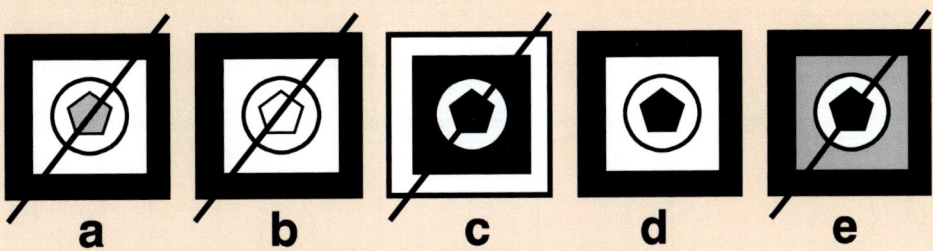

It is important to **eliminate** the wrong possibilities:

a - The Pentagon has a Grey Fill.
b - The Pentagon has a White Fill.
c - The fills of the two outer shapes have not been reversed.
e - The fills of the two outer shapes have not been reversed.

The Correct Figure:

The matrix follows the analogy rules.

Layer 1 - The fills of the two outer shapes reverse: Black goes to White and White goes to Black.

Layer 2 - The Grey Fill in the Pentagon becomes Black.

Answer: **d**

Exercise 12: 2

Which figure on the right completes the matrix?

Note: If the shapes in a row or column are of the same type, establish the rules in that direction.

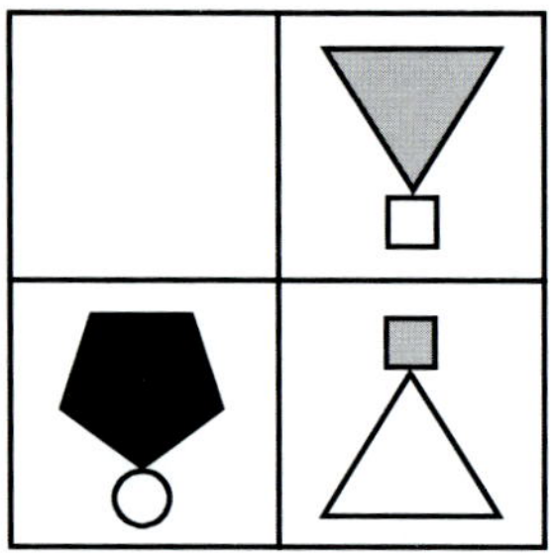

Answer ____

1) Matrix Rules: This matrix is best solved *vertically*.
   i) The whole figure reflects (or rotates 180°).
   ii) The fills swap.

Answer ____

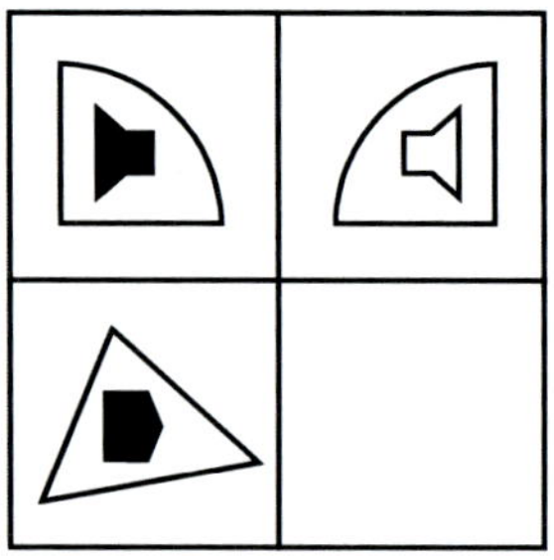

2) Matrix Rules: This matrix is best solved *horizontally*.
   i) _____
   ii) _____

Answer ____

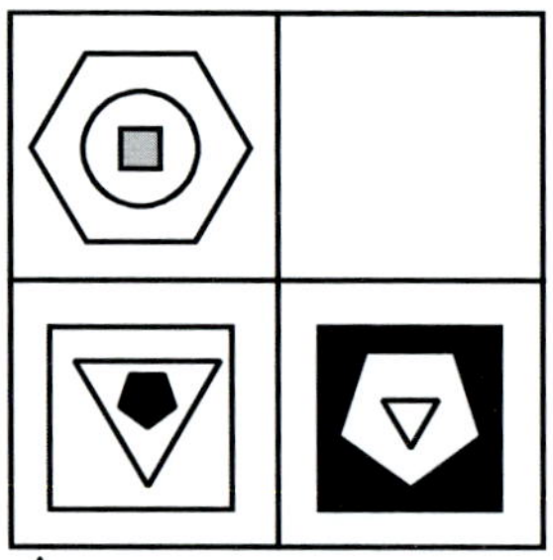

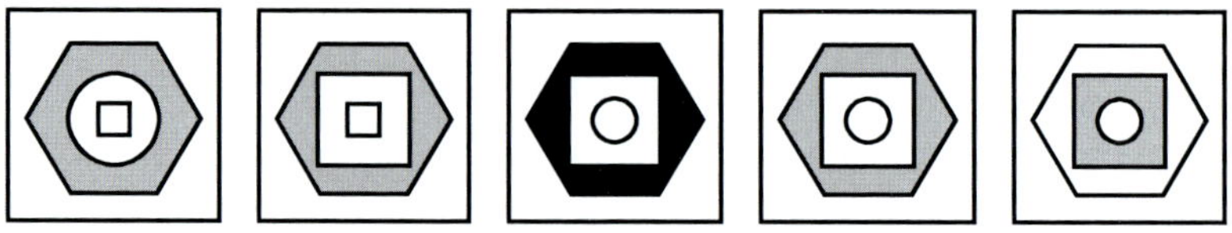

3) Matrix Rules: This matrix is best solved _____.
   i) _____
   ii) _____

Answer ____

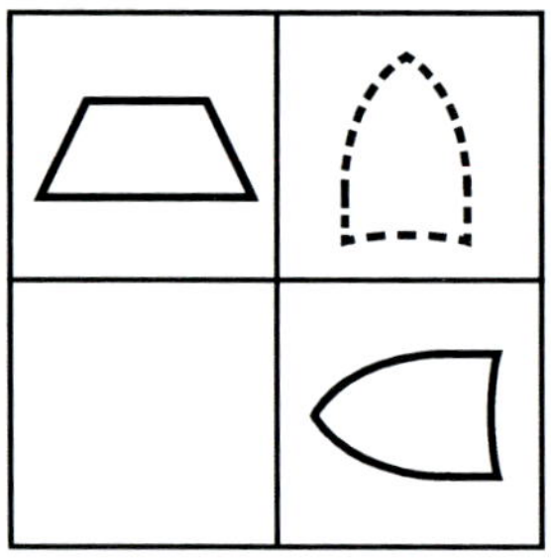

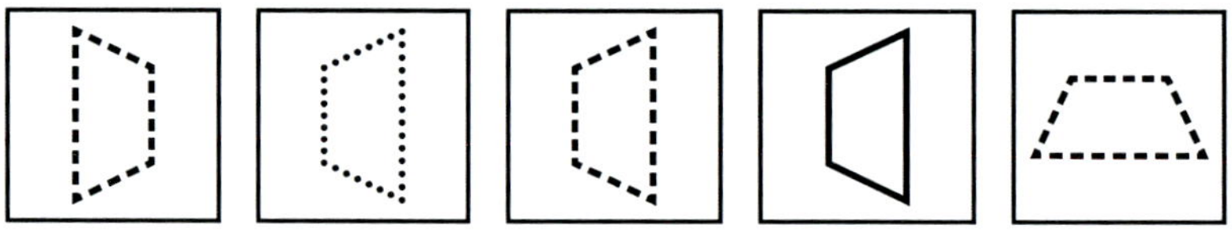

4) Matrix Rules: This matrix is best solved _____.
   i) _____
   ii) _____

Answer ____

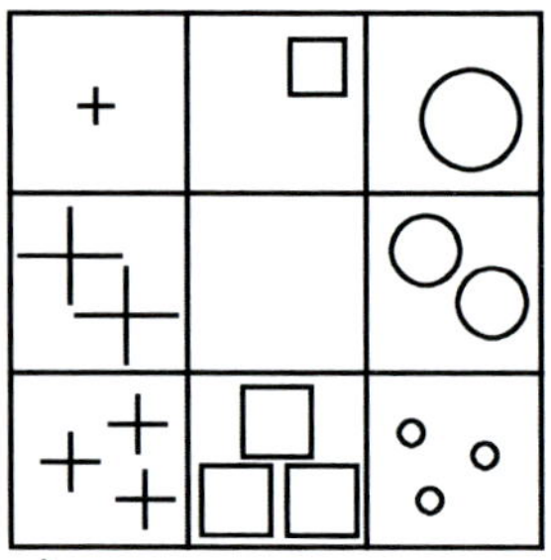

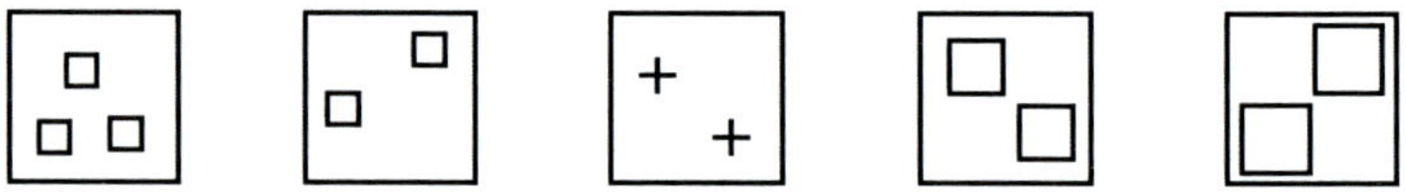

5) Matrix Rules: This matrix is best solved _____.
   i) _____
   ii) _____

© 2012 Stephen Curran

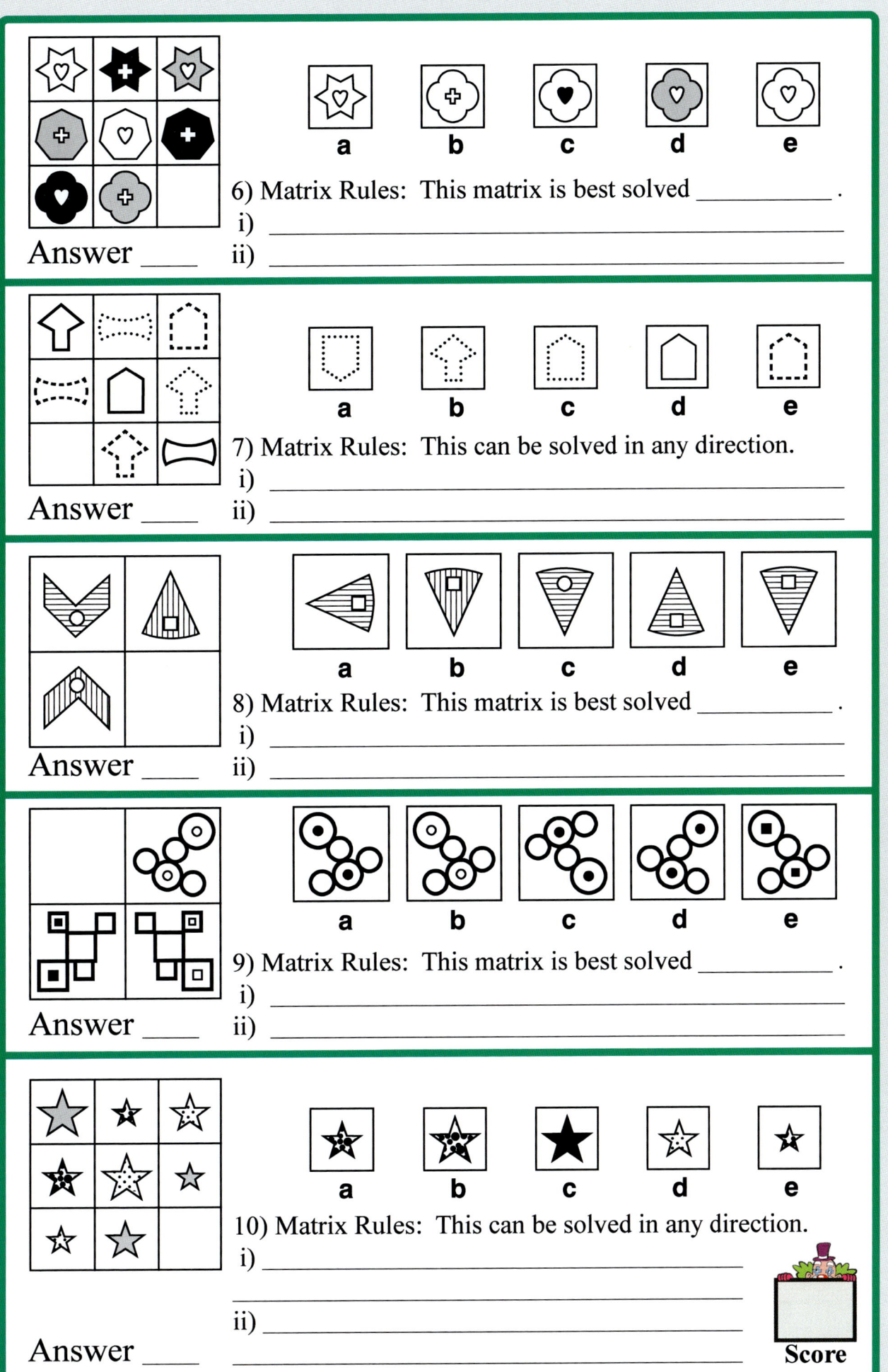

Chapter Thirteen
REVISION
1. Odd One Out

Exercise 13: 1 Which figure is the odd one out?

1) a b c d e

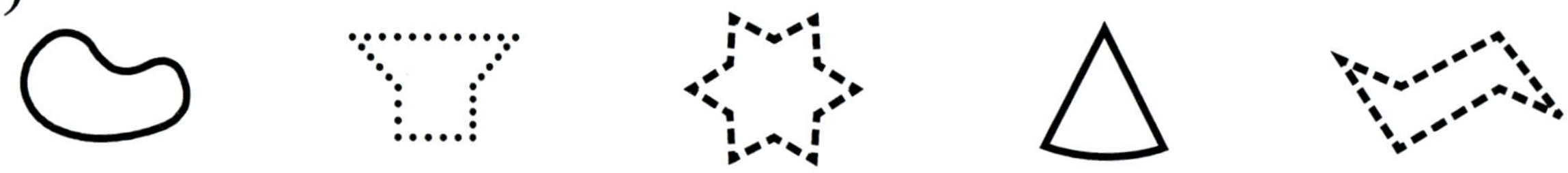

Answer ____

2) a b c d e

Answer ____

3) a b c d e

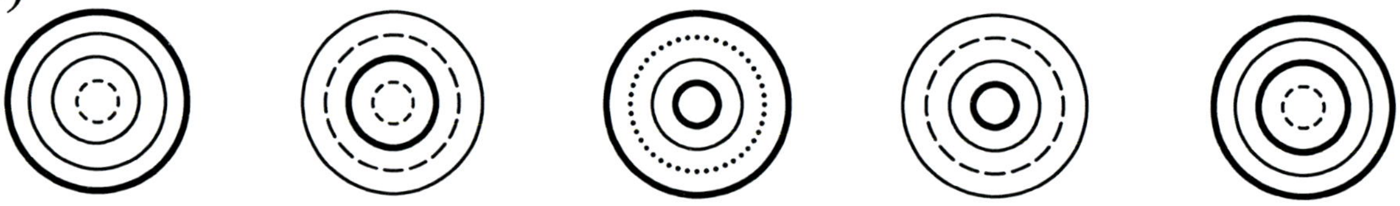

Answer ____

4) a b c d e

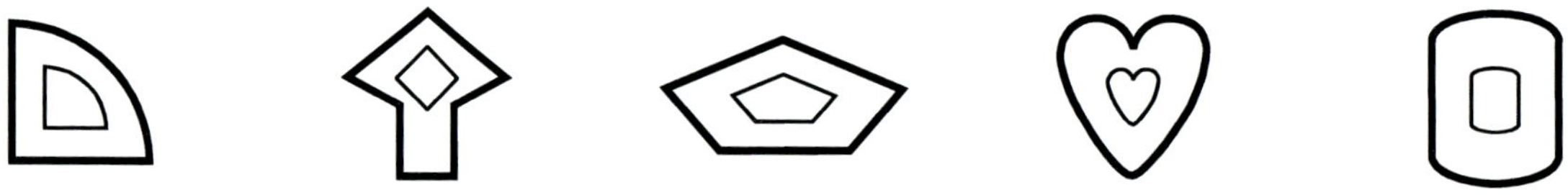

Answer ____

5) a b c d e

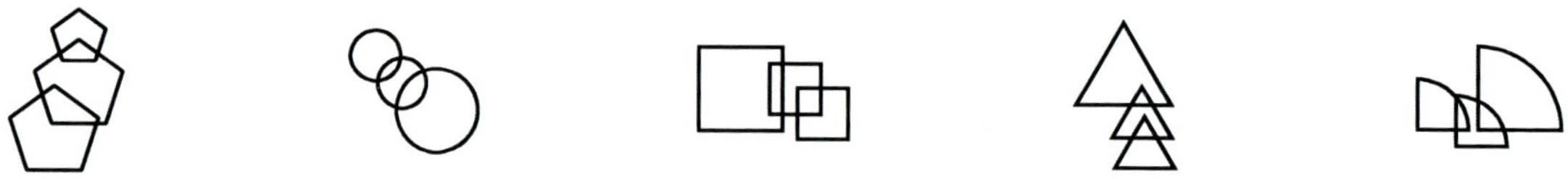

Answer ____

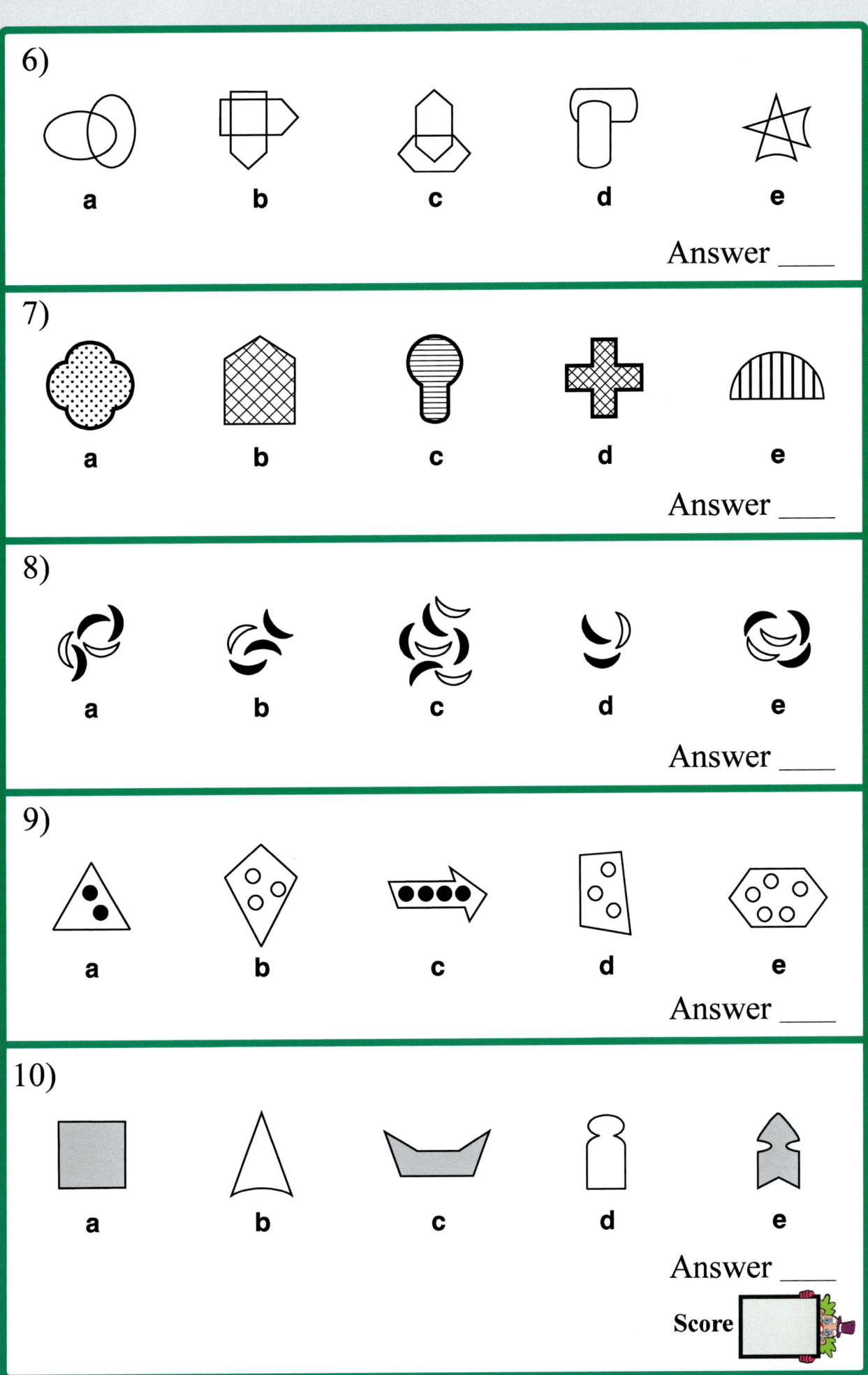

2. Codes

Exercise 13: 2 — Which set of letters on the right represents the Test Figure?

1)
Key		Test Figure	a	b	c	d	e
	LA		NC	MA	NB	MC	NA
	MB						
	LC						
	ND						

Answer ____

2)
Key		Test Figure	a	b	c	d	e
	XE		XF	YF	ZE	XY	EX
	YE						
	ZF						

Answer ____

3)
Key		Test Figure	a	b	c	d	e
	PS		PT	QS	PU	PQ	ST
	QT						
	QU						

Answer ____

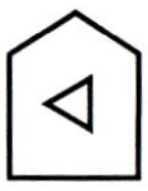

4)
Key		Test Figure	a	b	c	d	e
	FV		FW	FG	HW	VW	GH
	GW						
	HV						

Answer ____

5)
Key		Test Figure	a	b	c	d	e
	RJ		SK	RL	TK	SL	TJ
	RK						
	SJ						
	TL						

Answer ____

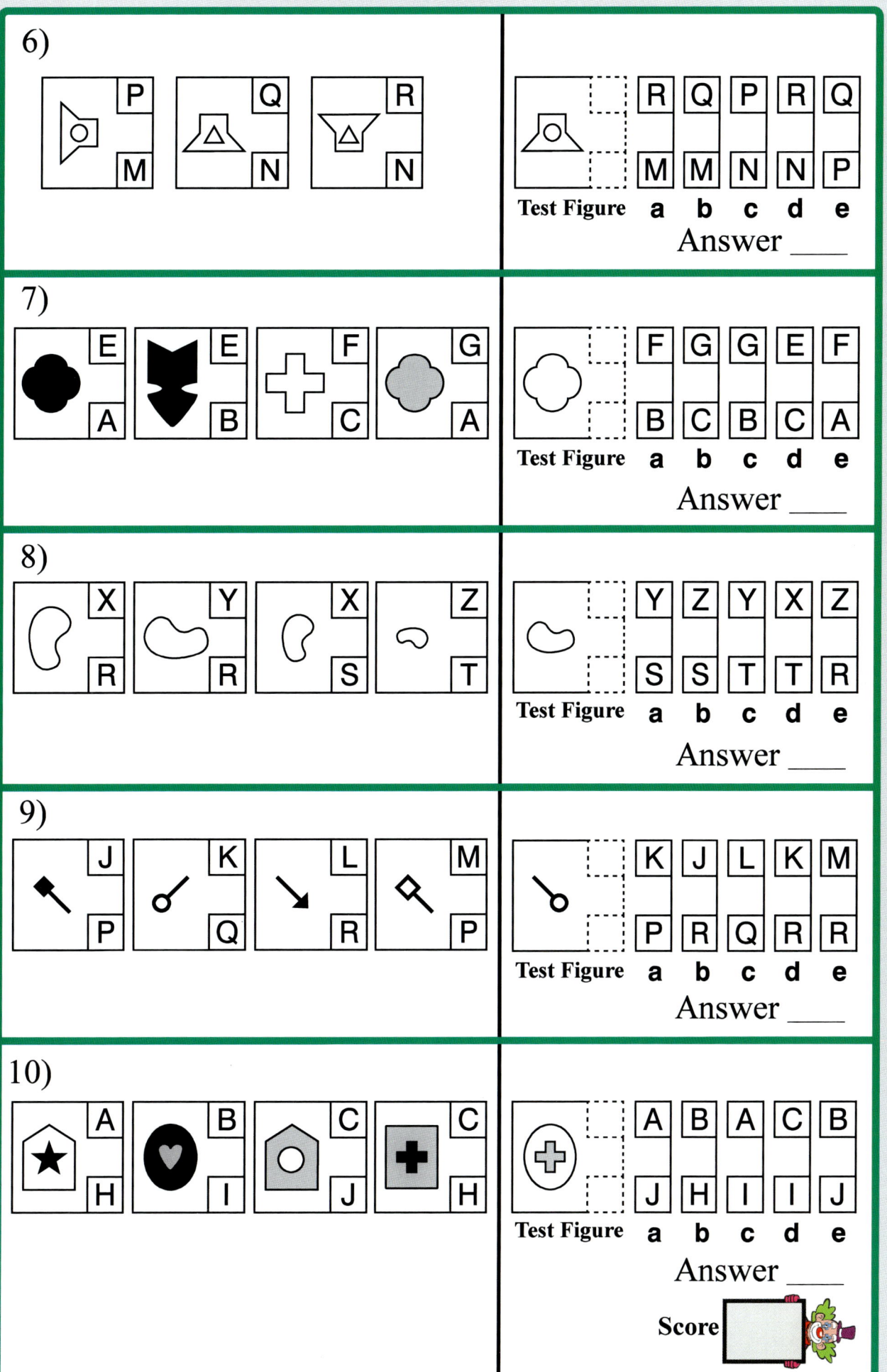

3. Analogies

Exercise 13: 3 Which figure completes the analogy?

1) Level 1 — Answer ____

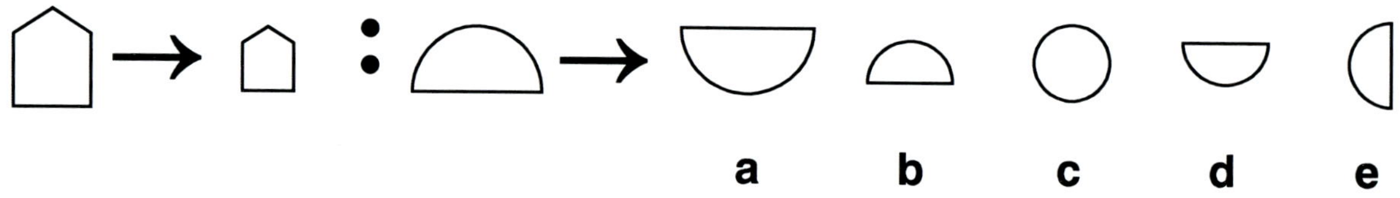

2) Level 1 — Answer ____

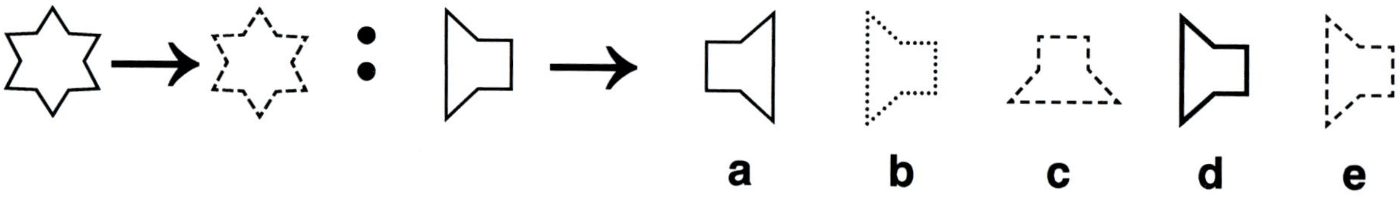

3) Level 2 — Answer ____

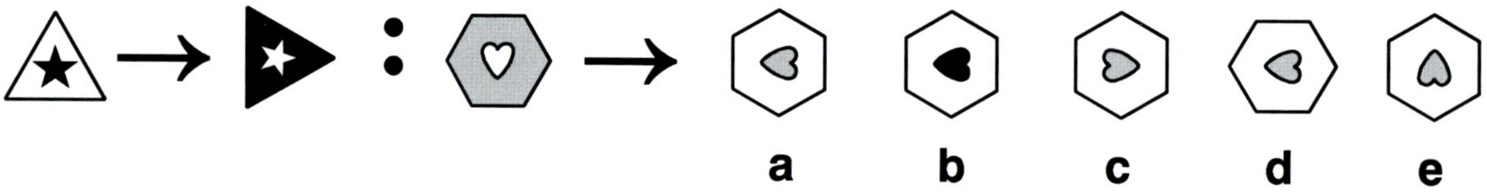

4) Level 2 — Answer ____

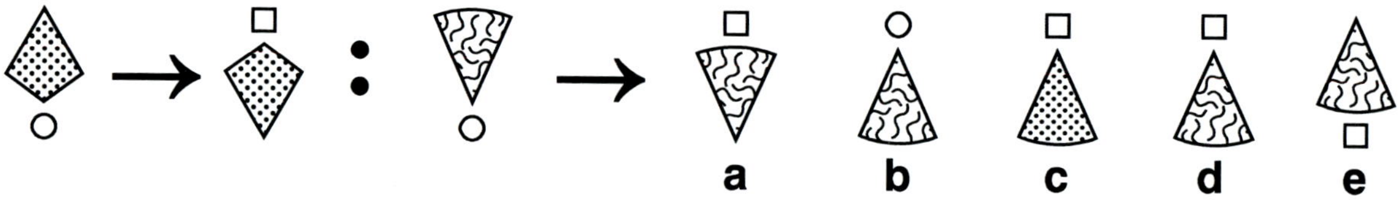

5) Level 1 — Answer ____

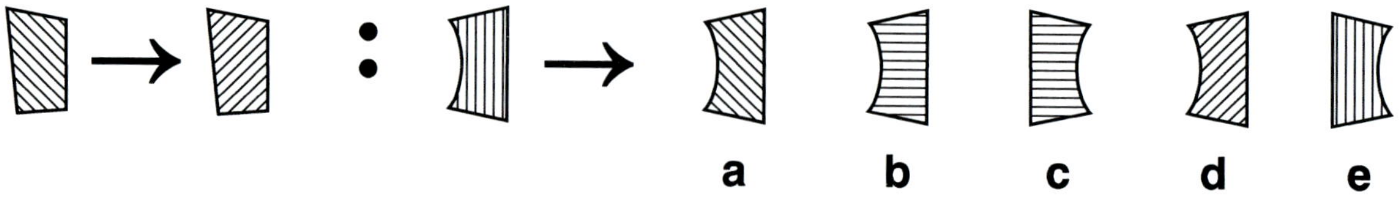

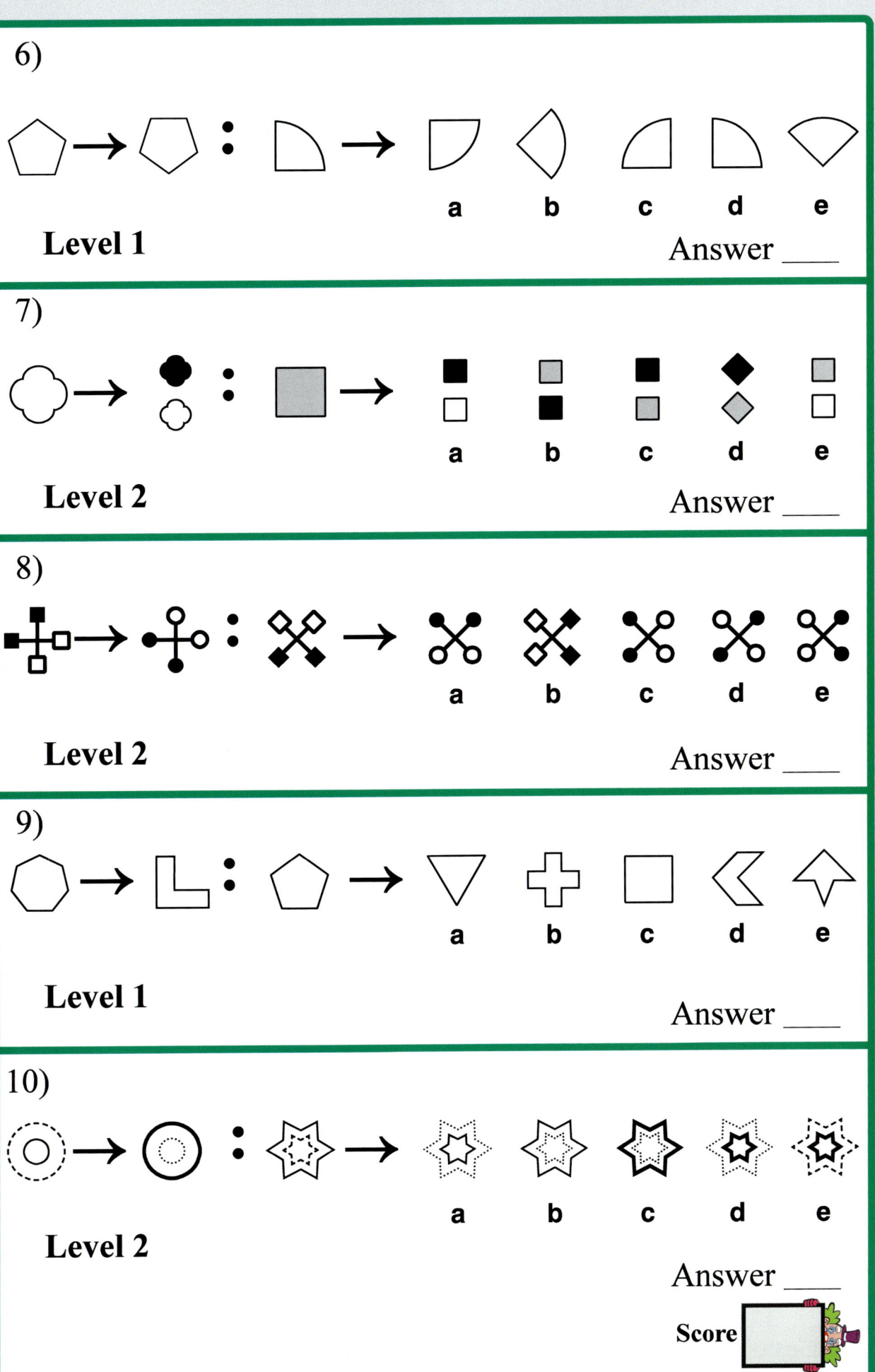

4. Similarities

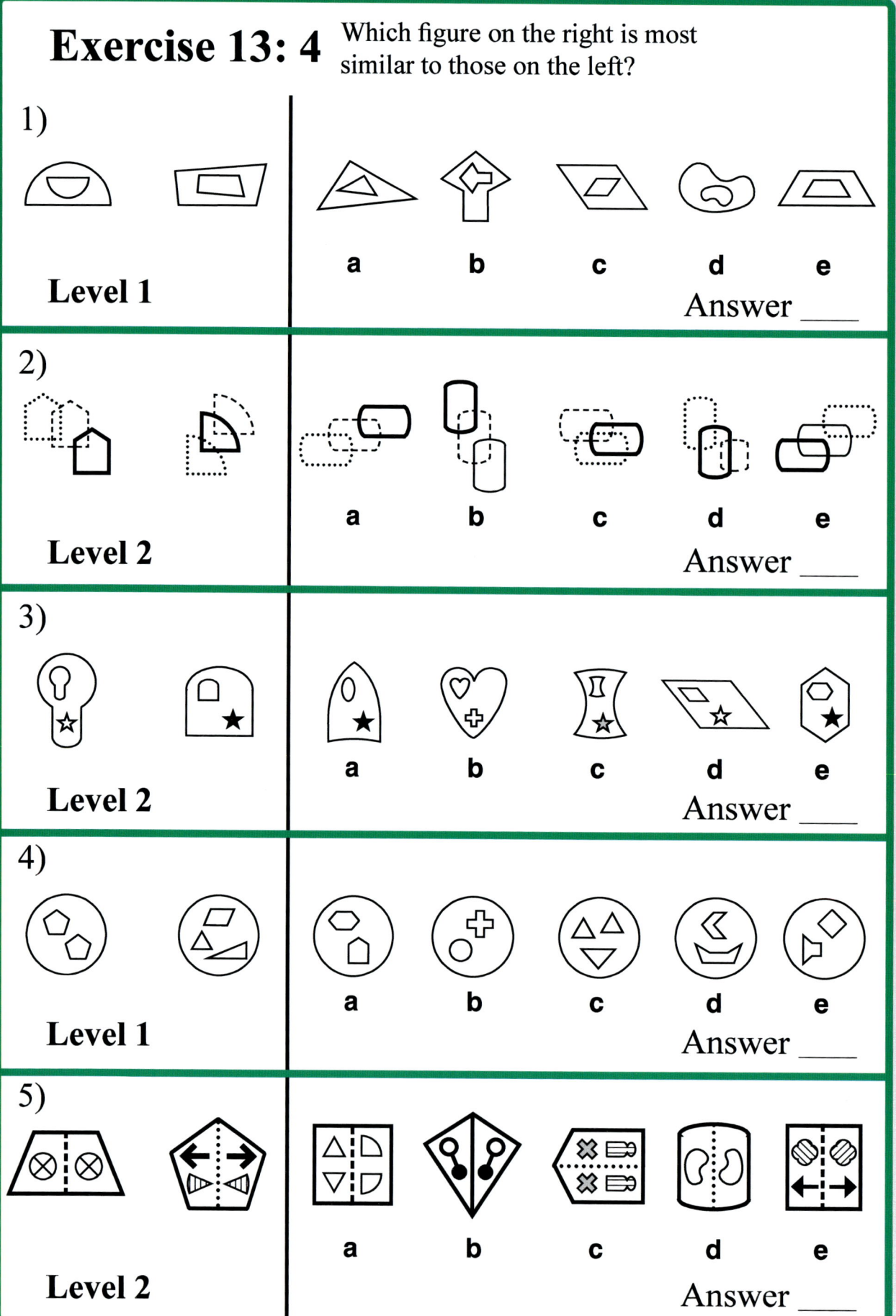

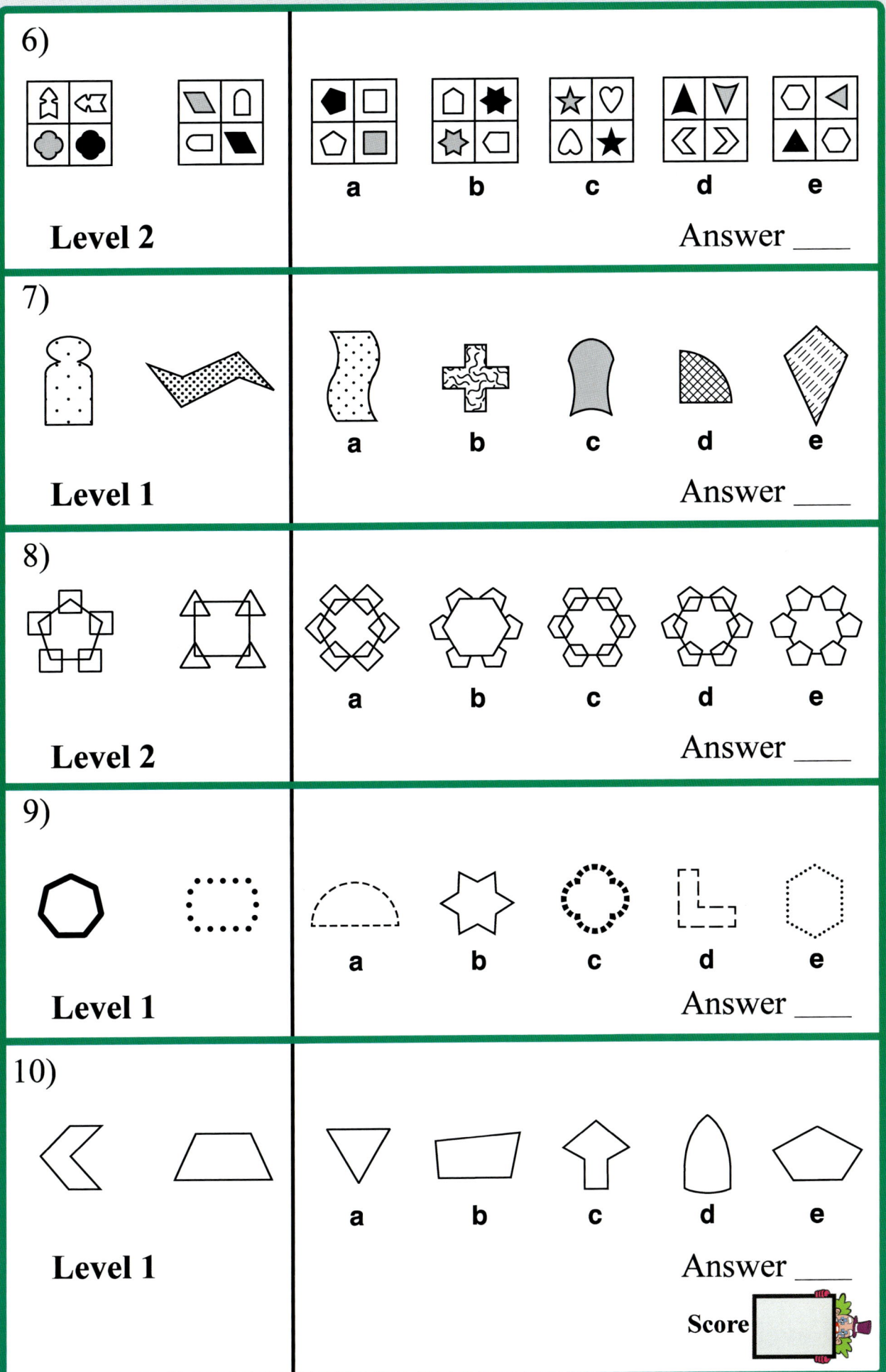

5. Series

Exercise 13: 5

Which figure on the right completes the series on the left?

1)

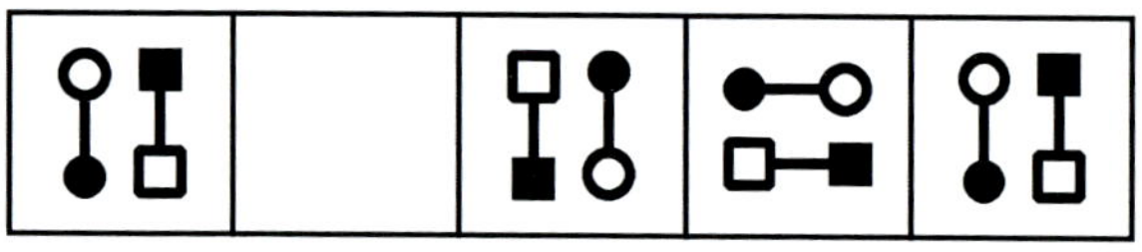

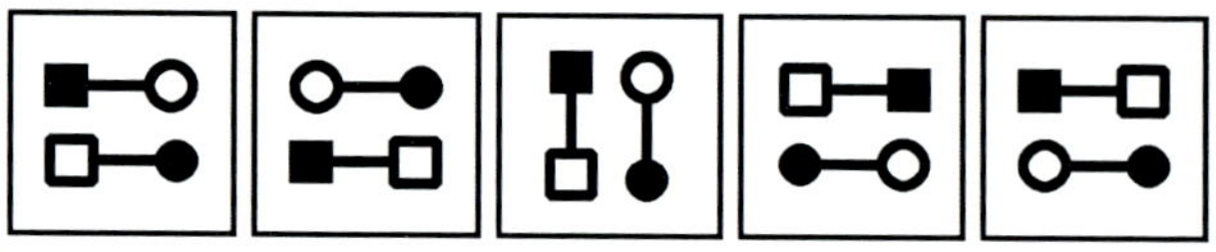

a b c d e

Level 1

Answer ____

2)

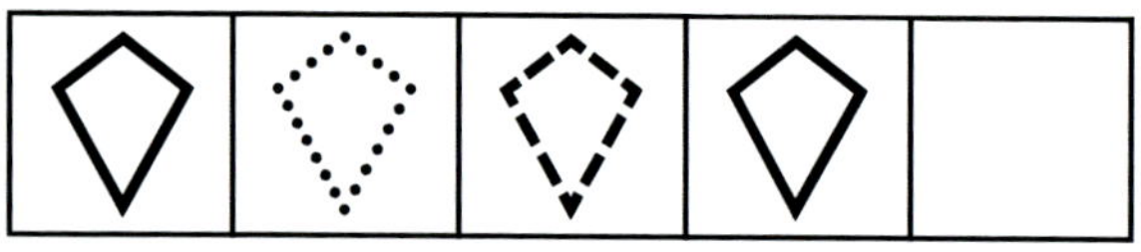

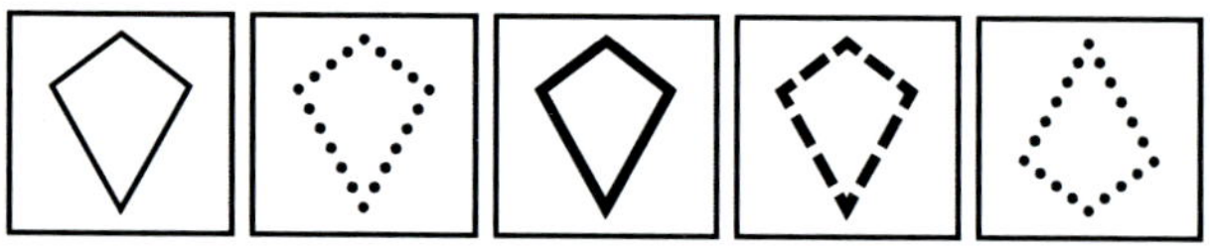

a b c d e

Level 1

Answer ____

3)

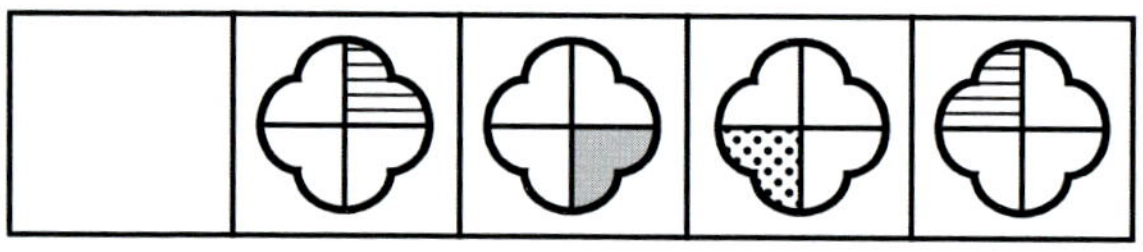

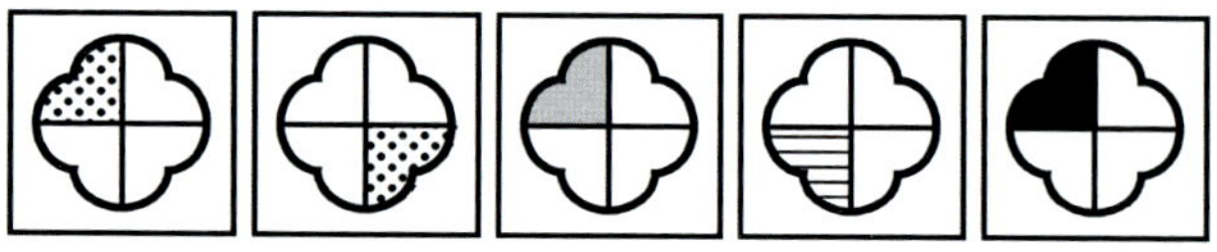

a b c d e

Level 2

Answer ____

4)

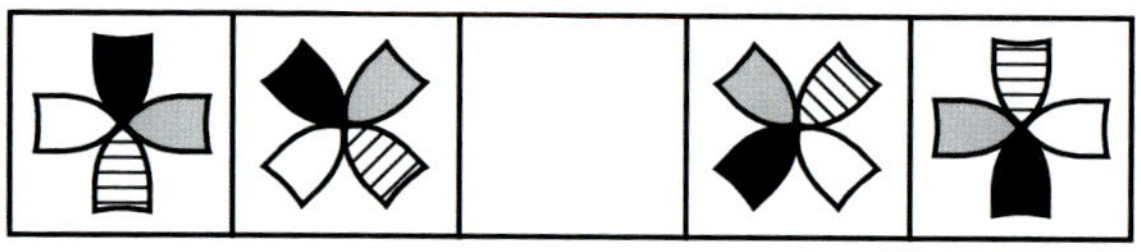

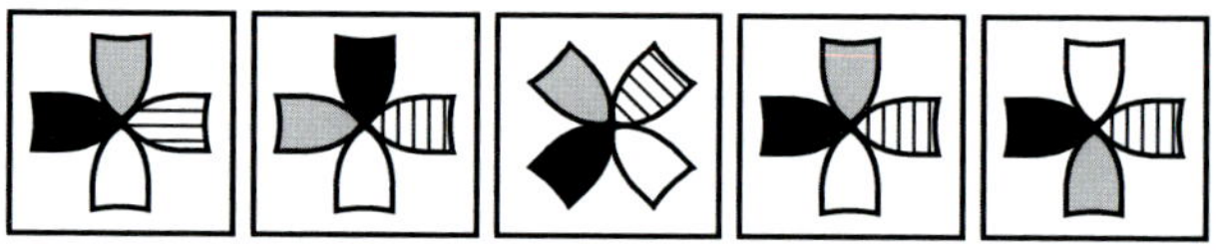

a b c d e

Level 1

Answer ____

5)

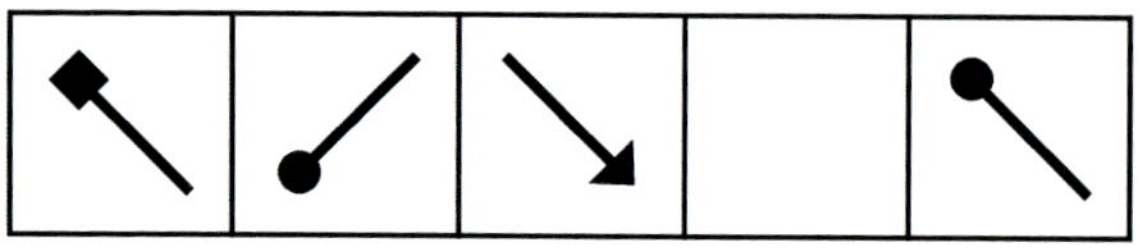

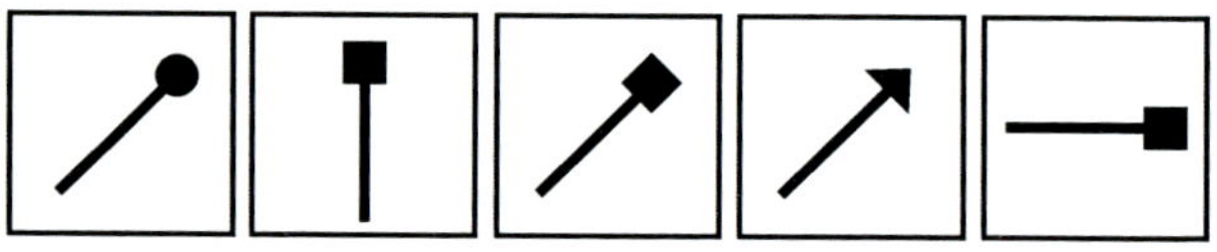

a b c d e

Level 2

Answer ____

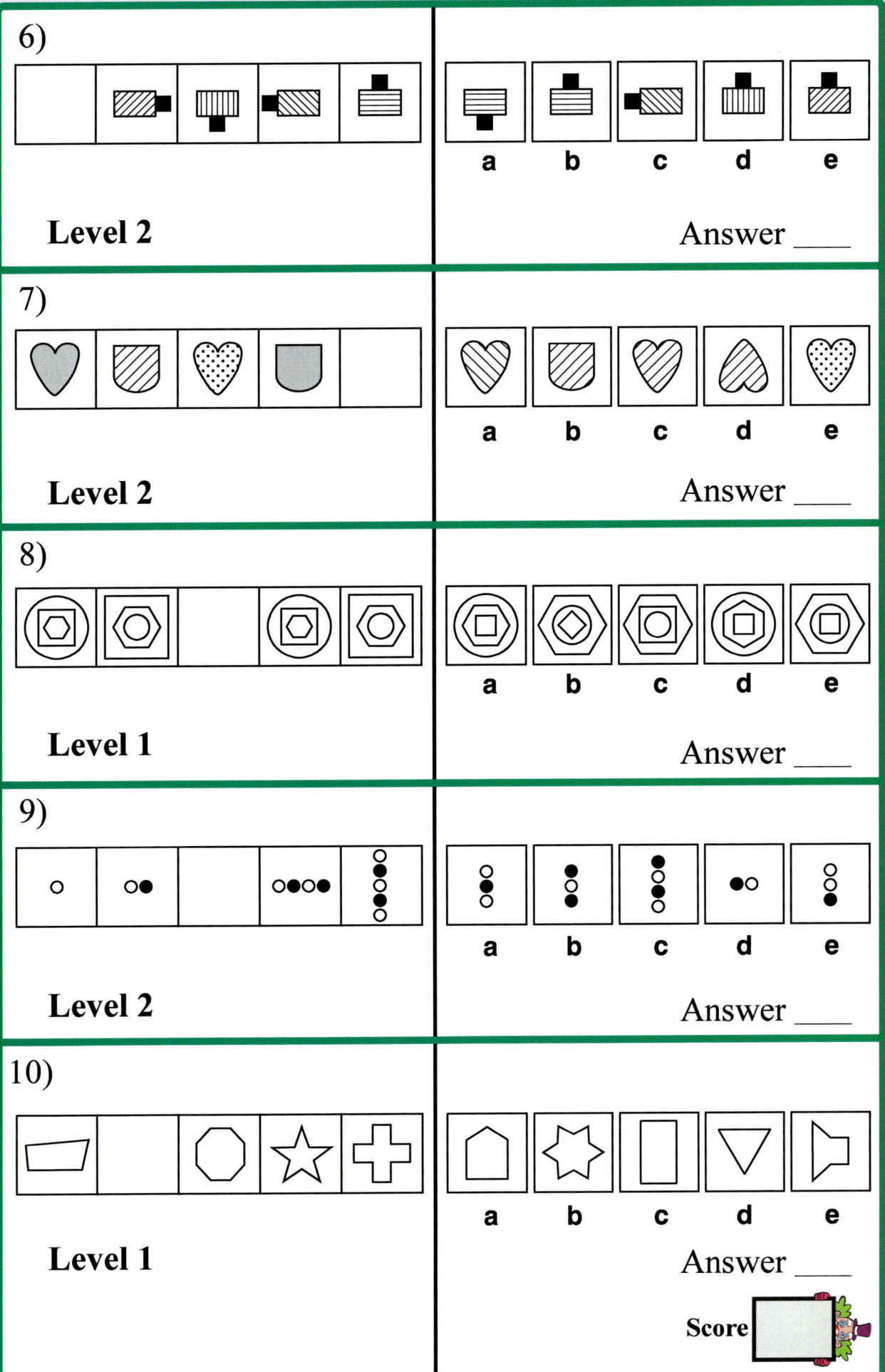

6. Matrices

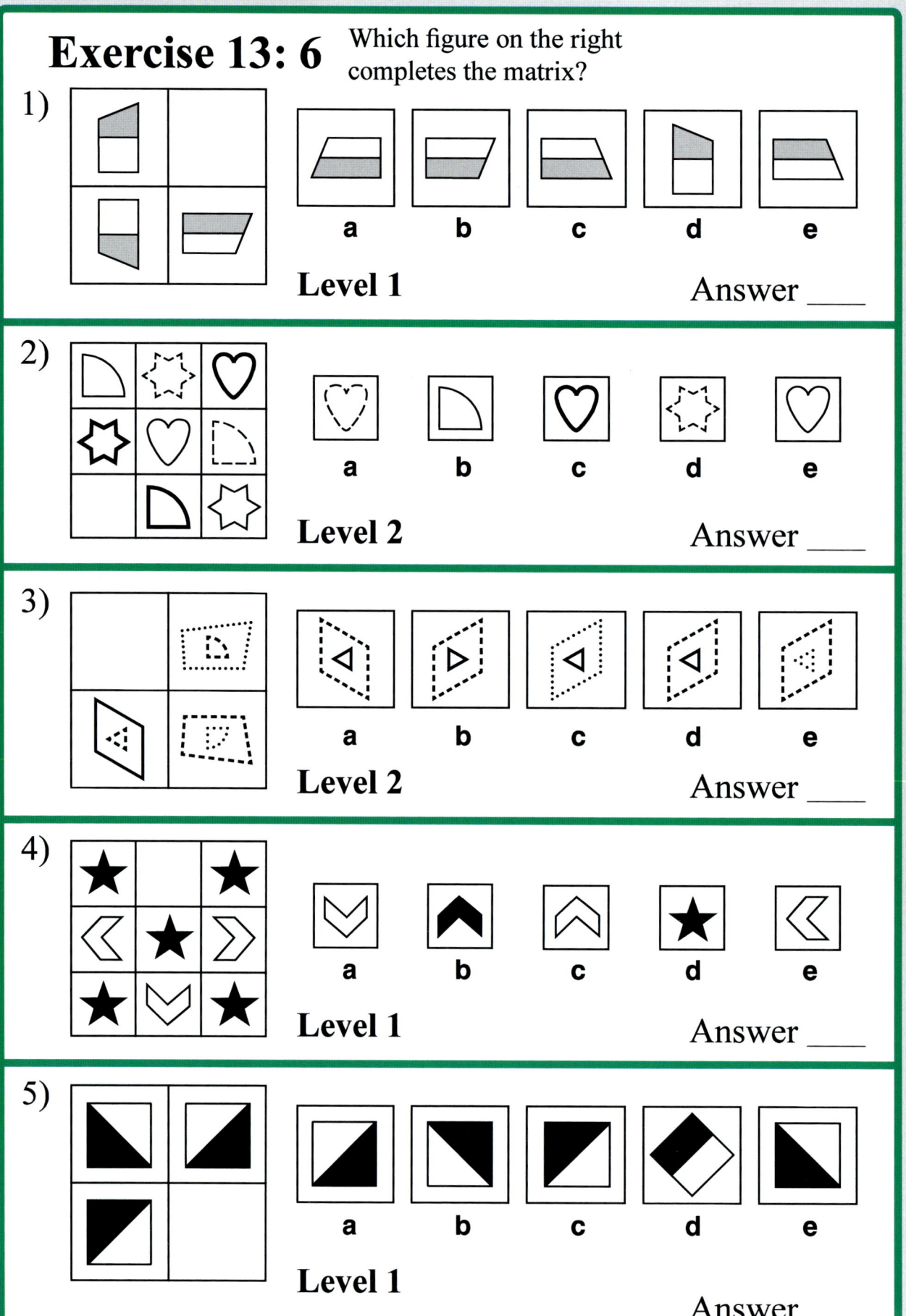

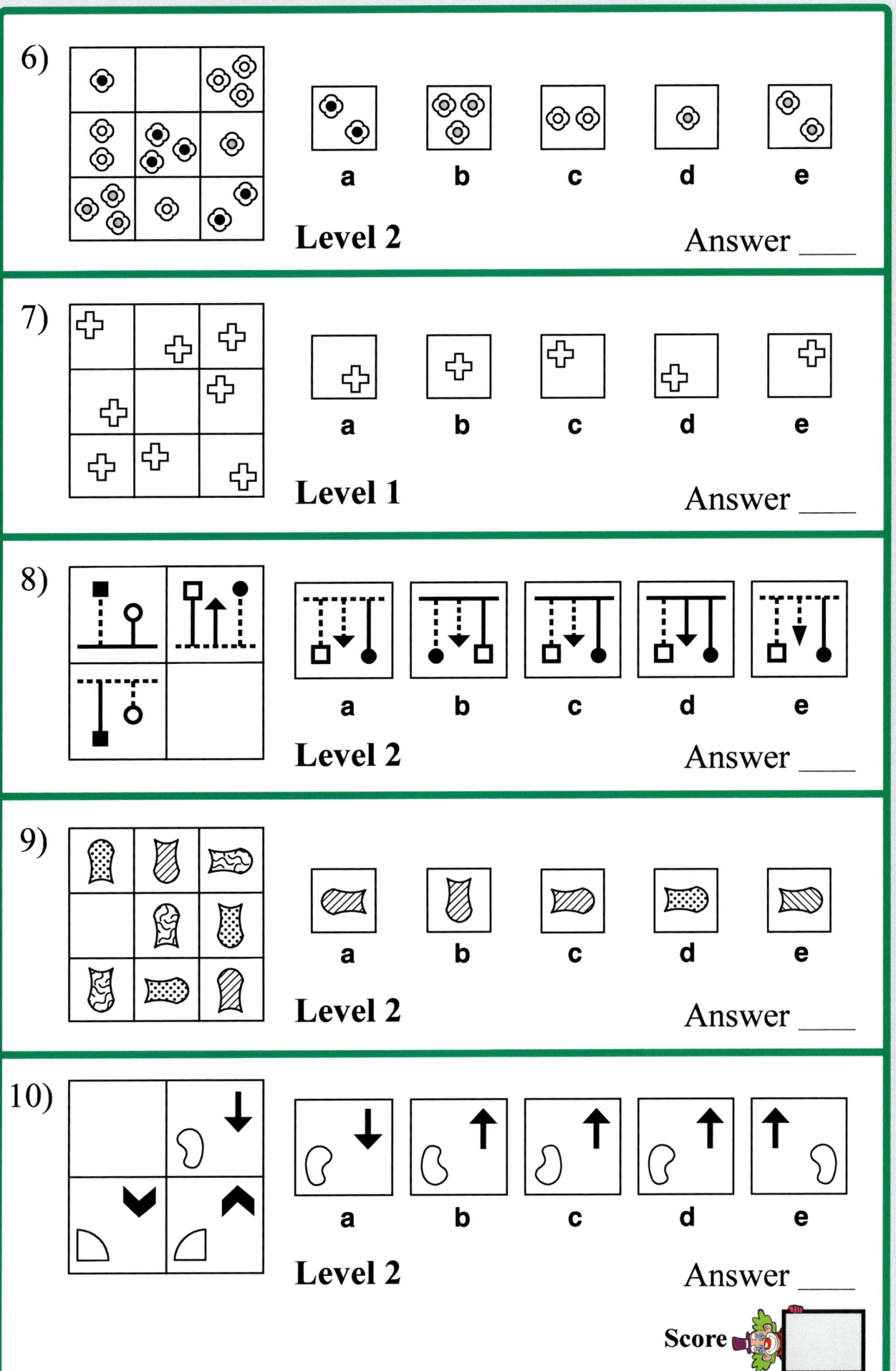

Notes

Answers

11+ Non-verbal Reasoning
Year 3/4 Workbook 2

Chapter Seven
Odd One Out
Exercise 7: 1
1) **e** - The Circle is not the same size as the other Circles.
2) **d** - The figure has two Black Filled Squares, not three.
3) **a** - The small Grey Shape is not an overlay.
4) **c** - The figure has a Slant Shaded Fill, not a Horizontal or Vertical Shaded Fill.
5) **d** - The figure is not divided into an even number of parts.
6) **b** - The Lines do not run from vertex to vertex, creating unequal segments.
7) **e** - There is not one more Flower Shape than Stars.
8) **a** - The shape points left, not upwards or right.
9) **d** - The figure is not a rotation but an inversion of the other figures.
10) **c** - The frequency (number) of Crosses and Small House Shapes do not equal each other.

Chapter Eight
Codes
Exercise 8: 1
1) **d**
   i) D - Grey Fill; E - Black Fill
   ii) Y - Large Cross; Z - Small Cross
2) **a**
   i) S - Flower - Solid Line;
      T - Flower - Dashed Line
   ii) P - Circle with Black Fill;
       Q - Circle with White Fill
3) **c**
   i) A - Arrow pointing downwards;
      B - Arrow pointing right;
      C - Arrow pointing left
   ii) J - Speckled Fill; K - White Fill
4) **e**
   i) G - Circle;
      H - Pentagon
   ii) R - Enclosed Triangle;
       S - Enclosed Square
5) **e**
   i) O - Heart Shape;
      P - Star
   ii) W - Horizontal Shaded Fill;
       X - Cross-hatched Fill;
       Y - Mottled Fill
6) **c**
   i) V - Speaker facing left;
      W - Speaker facing right
   ii) A - Black Fill; B - White Fill;
       C - Grey Fill
7) **c**
   i) Q - Sector;
      R - Semi-circle;
      S - Ellipse
   ii) K - Left Slant Shaded Fill;
       L - Horizontal Shaded Fill
8) **a**
   i) F - Two Lines perpendicular to each other;
      G - Vertical Line;
      H - Horizontal Line
   ii) P - Large Octagon;
       Q - Small Octagon
9) **d**
   i) U - Arrow facing upwards;
      V - Arrow facing left
   ii) I - Star; J - Heart Shape;
       K - Shield Shape

11+ Non-verbal Reasoning Year 3/4 Workbook 2

Answers

10) **b**
  i) W - Arrow facing upwards;
    X - Arrow facing right;
    Y - Arrow facing downwards;
    Z - Arrow facing left
  ii) S - Large Arrow;
    T - Small Arrow

Exercise 8: 2

1) **e**
  i) E - Circles;
    F - Squares;
    G - Hexagons
  ii) Y - Three shapes; Z - Two shapes

2) **b**
  i) A - Circle with Black Fill;
    B - Circle with Grey Fill
  ii) S - Speaker Shape facing left;
    T - Speaker Shape facing downwards;
    U - Speaker Shape facing upwards

3) **e**
  i) J - Cross at the bottom;
    K - Cross at the top;
    L - Cross at the middle
  ii) N - Vertical Shaded Fill;
    O - White Fill

4) **d**
  i) C - Solid Thin Line;
    D - Dashed Thick Line;
    E - Solid Thick Line
  ii) P - Vertical Ellipse;
    Q - Horizontal Ellipse

5) **a**
  i) F - Circle with Black Fill;
    G - Circle with White Fill;
    H - Circle with Grey Fill
  ii) L - No enclosed shapes;
    M - Enclosed shapes

6) **c**
  i) S - Hexagon;
    T - Pentagon
  ii) J - White Fill;
    K - Grey Fill;
    L - Black Fill

7) **d**
  i) A - Circle;
    B - Square;
    C - Triangle
  ii) L - Right Slant Solid Shaded Fill;
    M - Cross-hatched Fill;
    N - Vertical Dashed Shaded Fill

8) **b**
  i) U - Large Triangle;
    V - Medium Triangle;
    W - Small Triangle
  ii) G - Triangle facing upwards;
    H - Triangle facing left;
    I - Triangle facing downwards

9) **a**
  i) P - Top right Fill;
    Q - Bottom left Fill;
    R - Top left Fill
  ii) J - Grey Fill;
    K - Vertical Shaded Fill;
    L - Black Fill;
    M - Right Slant Shaded Fill

10) **c**
  i) X - Lattice Fill;
    Y - Dotted Fill;
    Z - Horizontal Shaded Fill
  ii) E - Sector facing right;
    F - Sector facing upwards;
    G - Sector facing downwards

Chapter Nine
Analogies
Exercise 9: 1

1) **a** - The shape has been rotated 180°.
2) **c** - The Triangles have been merged vertically.
3) **b** - The small linked shapes have been rotated 45°.

Answers

11+ Non-verbal Reasoning
Year 3/4 Workbook 2

4) **d** - Only the linked parts of the two shapes have remained.
5) **b** - The fills have been swapped.
6) **a** - The shape has been stretched horizontally.
7) **c** - The shapes have changed places.
8) **b** - The shape has been reflected horizontally.
9) **e** - The Speaker Shape has become a Churn Shape with the same type of outline.
10) **d** - The Solid and Dashed Outlines have swapped.

Exercise 9: 2
1) **d**
 i) The shape has been rotated 90°.
 ii) The same shape with a Grey Fill has been added.
2) **b**
 i) An identical shape reflected, or rotated 180°, has been added.
 ii) The two shapes have been merged.
3) **c**
 i) The original shape has been enclosed by a larger version of the same shape.
 ii) A Black Fill has been added to the enclosed shape.
4) **c**
 i) The figure has been rotated 90° clockwise.
 ii) The figure has been reduced.
5) **a**
 i) The figure has been reflected vertically or rotated 90° anticlockwise.
 ii) The line types have been swapped.
6) **a**
 i) The Shaded Fills have been rotated 90°.

 ii) The figure has been enlarged.
7) **d**
 i) The figure has been flipped/inverted vertically or rotated 180°.
 ii) The Line has been changed from Thick to Thin.
8) **e**
 i) The Lines of the outer shape have been changed from Dashed to Solid.
 ii) The enclosed shape has been changed from a Black Fill to a White Fill.
9) **c**
 i) The Shaded Fill has been rotated 90°.
 ii) The shape has been enclosed by another shape of the same type.
10) **a**
 i) The large shape has been rotated 90° anticlockwise.
 ii) The small shape has been vertically transposed.

Chapter Ten
Similarities
Exercise 10: 1
1) **e** - The shape is Straight-edged.
2) **b** - The shape has a Horizontal Shaded Fill.
3) **d** - The large shape encloses a Cross with a Black Fill.
4) **c** - The shape has only one Curved Side.
5) **e** - The shape has an Arrowhead Ending.
6) **c** - The shape has six sides.
7) **d** - The enclosure is a Heart Shape.
8) **b** - The shape has a Dotted Fill.
9) **b** - There is one ending with a Black Fill.

Answers

11+ Non-verbal Reasoning Year 3/4 Workbook 2

10) **a** - The shape has one line of symmetry.

Exercise 10: 2
1) **e**
   i) The outer shape has a Dotted Outline.
   ii) The enclosed shape has a Thick Solid Outline.
2) **e**
   i) The Star has a Black Fill.
   ii) The Star overlays the Ellipse.
3) **a**
   i) There are four Squares.
   ii) There are two Circles.
4) **d**
   i) There are three small shapes.
   ii) One small shape is an overlay; two small shapes are linkages.
5) **c**
   i) There are the same number of Circles as the large shape has sides.
   ii) One of the Circles has a Black Fill.
6) **b**
   i) The shape is divided in half from corner to corner.
   ii) The dividing Line is Dotted or Dashed.
7) **d**
   i) The top shape rotates 90° clockwise.
   ii) One shape has a Black Fill and one shape has a White Fill.
8) **a**
   i) There are three shapes of different sizes.
   ii) There is only one overlay.
9) **e**
   i) The outer figure is the same.
   ii) The enclosed shape has four sides.
10) **c**
    i) The outer shape has a Thick Solid Outline; the inner shape has a Dotted Outline.
    ii) The fills of the enclosed shapes are Grey and White, or Black and White.

Chapter Eleven
Series
Exercise 11: 1
1) **e** - The Quadrant and Star alternate at each stage; Repetitive.
2) **a** - The shading rotates 45° anticlockwise at each stage; Repetitive.
3) **c** - One clockwise vertex is added at each stage to build the Star; Cumulative.
4) **b** - The fills alternate Black, White, Grey at each stage; Repetitive.
5) **d** - A change in frequency occurs - shape sides increase by one at each stage; Cumulative.
6) **d** - The shape rotates 90° clockwise at each stage; Repetitive.
7) **b** - All the fills rotate clockwise at each stage; Repetitive.
8) **a** - The Circle enlarges, then reduces and then enlarges; Repetitive.
9) **e** - A Black Triangle is added in the corner at each stage; Cumulative.
10) **d** - The figure rotates 45° anticlockwise at each stage; Repetitive.

Exercise 11: 2
1) **b**
   i) The shape rotates 90° anticlockwise.
   ii) The fills alternate Solid, Liquid, Dotted, etc. at each stage.

Answers

11+ Non-verbal Reasoning Year 3/4 Workbook 2

2) **d**
  i) The figure alternates between vertical and horizontal at each stage.
  ii) The overlay shapes alternate in position: top, middle, bottom, middle, top, etc.

3) **c**
  i) The two Black Squares rotate clockwise by one space each time.
  ii) One White Square is removed at each stage.

4) **a**
  i) The Flower Shape rotates anticlockwise around the Square.
  ii) The Grey Circle rotates clockwise around the Square.

5) **e**
  i) The Cross rotates 45° at each stage.
  ii) One Arrow is added on the left at each stage.

6) **d**
  i) The Chevron Shape rotates 90° clockwise.
  ii) The background fill rotates 90° or alternates between Left Slant and Right Slant Shaded.

7) **a**
  i) The Pentagon is positioned: centre, right, centre, left, centre, etc.
  ii) The Star is positioned: bottom, middle, top, middle, bottom, etc.

8) **c**
  i) The shapes in each pair of figures change places.
  ii) The new outside shape rotates 180°.

9) **c**
  i) One Circle is filled with Black from the left at each stage.
  ii) One Line is added to the Bone Shape at the top or bottom alternately at each stage.

10) **b**
  i) The figure rotates 90° anticlockwise at each stage.
  ii) The fills swap places at each stage.

Chapter Twelve
Matrices
Exercise 12: 1

1) **e** - Solved vertically: The shape reduces and keeps its fill.

2) **b** - Solved horizontally: The fill changes from Grey to Black.
  or
  Solved vertically: The Cross becomes a Sector.

3) **a** - Solved vertically: The shape reflects across a horizontal line of reflective symmetry.

4) **a** - Solved horizontally: The shape rotates 90° anticlockwise.

5) **d** - Solved horizontally, vertically or diagonally.
  Solved horizontally or vertically: The shape types alternate.
  or
  Solved left or right diagonally: The shapes are the same in each diagonal line.

6) **c** - Solved horizontally, vertically or diagonally.
  Solved horizontally, vertically or left diagonally: There is one of each shape in each line.
  or
  Solved right diagonally: The shapes are the same.

7) **d** - Solved vertically: A horizontal line of reflective symmetry can be drawn through the middle of the matrix.

Answers

8) **b** - Solved diagonally: A left or right diagonal line of reflective symmetry can be drawn through the matrix.
9) **e** - Solved horizontally: The figure rotates 90° clockwise.
10) **a** - Solved vertically: The shape reflects in a vertical direction at each stage.

Exercise 12: 2
1) **a** - Solved vertically:
   i) The figure reflects (or rotates 180°).
   ii) The fills swap.
2) **d** - Solved horizontally:
   i) The figure reflects.
   ii) The fill in the enclosed shape changes from Black to White.
3) **d** - Solved horizontally:
   i) The inner two shapes change places.
   ii) The outer shape takes the fill of the inner shape.
4) **c** - Solved vertically:
   i) The shape rotates 90° anticlockwise.
   ii) The Dotted Outlines become Solid and the Solid Outlines become Dotted.
5) **b** - Solved vertically:
   i) The number of Crosses, Squares or Circles is 1, 2, 3 from top to bottom.
   ii) There are three sizes of each shape: small, medium, large.
6) **e** - Solved horizontally:
   i) The enclosed shapes alternate Cross, Heart Shape, Cross, etc.
   ii) The outer shape in each column must have one of each fill: Grey, White, Black.
7) **c** - Solve in either direction:
   i) There is one of each shape horizontally and vertically.
   ii) There is one of each type of line horizontally and vertically.
8) **e** - Solved vertically:
   i) The whole figure reflects (or rotates 180°).
   ii) The Shaded Fill rotates 90°.
9) **a** - Solved horizontally:
   i) The figure reflects horizontally.
   ii) The fills of the small shapes change from Black to White.
10) **b** - Solve in any direction
    i) There must be a small, medium and large Star Shape both vertically and horizontally.
    ii) There is one of each fill type in each line: Solid, Liquid, Dotted.

Chapter Thirteen
Revision
Exercise 13: 1
1) **b** - The shape does not have a Dashed or a Solid Outline.
2) **d** - The shape is not Straight-edged.
3) **c** - The figure does not have Solid and Dashed line types.
4) **b** - The enclosed shape is not the same as the outer shape.
5) **a** - The two shapes that are the same size are not the smallest shapes in the figure.
6) **d** - The shapes are not linked.
7) **a** - The shape does not have a Shaded or Cross-hatched Fill.
8) **b** - There is not one more Moon Shape with a Black Fill than with a White Fill.

Answers

11+ Non-verbal Reasoning Year 3/4 Workbook 2

9) **c** - The number of enclosed Circles is not equal to one less than the number of sides.
10) **a** - The shape does not have only one line of symmetry.

Exercise 13: 2
1) **e** - N - White Fill; A - Churn Shape points upwards
2) **a** - X - Square; F - Large figure
3) **c** - P - Bone Shape; U - Vertical Shaded Fill
4) **c** - H - House Shape; W - Triangle points left
5) **d** - S - Grey Fill; L - Kite points upwards
6) **b** - Q - Speaker faces downwards; M - Circle enclosed
7) **e** - F - White Fill; A - Flower Shape
8) **a** - Y - Orientation of the Bean Shape; S - Medium-sized Figure
9) **d** - K - Circle Line Ending; R - Line points bottom right
10) **c** - A - Outer shape has a White Fill; I - Inner shape has a Grey Fill

Exercise 13: 3
1) **b** - The shape has been reduced.
2) **e** - The line type has been changed from Solid to Dashed.
3) **a** - The figure has been rotated 90° clockwise. The fills have been swapped.
4) **d** - The figure has been flipped vertically. The Circle has become a Square.
5) **b** - The Shaded Fill has been rotated 90°.
6) **a** - The shape has been flipped vertically.
7) **c** - The shape has been reduced and has become the bottom shape. A duplicate with a Black Fill has become the top shape.
8) **e** - The figure has been rotated 90° anticlockwise. The Squares have become Circles.
9) **c** - One side has been subtracted.
10) **d** - The Dashed Line has become Thick Solid. The Thin Solid Line has become Dotted.

Exercise 13: 4
1) **c** - The inner shape is a vertical reflection of the outer shape.
2) **a** - Three identical shapes are linked to each other. There is one with a Thick Solid Outline, one with a Dashed Outline and one with a Dotted Outline.
3) **d** - There is a smaller replica of the outer shape enclosed at the top left of the figure. The outer shape is Curved.
4) **e** - The number of sides of the enclosed shapes totals 10.
5) **e** - The enclosed Vertical Line is a line of symmetry. The Line is either Dashed or Dotted.
6) **b** - There is a 90° anticlockwise rotation between the shapes with a White Fill. The shapes with a White Fill are the same and the shapes with Grey and Black Fills are the same.
7) **a** - The shape has a Dotted Fill.
8) **d** - There is one shape linked on each corner. The linked shapes have one less side than the larger shape.
9) **c** - The shape has a Thick Outline.

11+ Non-verbal Reasoning
Year 3/4 Workbook 2

Answers

10) **b** - The shape has an even number of sides.

Exercise 13: 5
1) **e** - The figure rotates 90° anticlockwise.
2) **b** - The order of line types is: Solid, Dotted, Dashed, Solid, Dotted.
3) **a** - The fill moves one section clockwise. The order of fills is: Dotted, Horizontal Shaded, Grey, Dotted, Horizontal Shaded.
4) **d** - The figure rotates 45° anticlockwise.
5) **c** - The figure rotates 90° anticlockwise. The order of line endings is: Square, Circle, Triangle, Square, Circle.
6) **b** - The Square with a Black Fill moves clockwise around the shape. The Shaded Fill rotates 45° anticlockwise.
7) **c** - The Heart Shape and Loaf Shape alternate. The order of fills is: Grey, Right Slant Shaded, Dotted, Grey, Right Slant Shaded.
8) **e** - The shapes move one position outwards.
9) **a** - One Circle is added with alternating Black and White Fills. The orientation alternates between horizontal and vertical.
10) **e** - Two sides are added.

Exercise 13: 6
1) **c** - Solved vertically: The figure flips along the horizontal mid-line of the matrix.
2) **a** - Solved vertically or horizontally: There is one Quadrant, one Star and one Heart Shape. There is one Thin Solid Outline, one Thick Solid Outline and one Dashed Outline.
3) **d** - Solved vertically: The figure flips along the horizontal mid-line of the matrix. The line types swap.
4) **c** - Solved as a whole: The matrix is symmetrical.
5) **b** - Solved as a whole: The matrix is symmetrical.
6) **e** - Solved vertically or horizontally: There is one square with one figure, one square with two figures, and one square with three figures. There is one Black Fill, one White Fill and one Grey Fill.
7) **b** - Solved vertically or horizontally: There is one shape in the top left corner, one shape in the bottom right corner and one shape in the middle.
8) **c** - Solved vertically: The figure flips along the horizontal mid-line of the matrix. The Solid and Dashed Lines swap.
9) **c** - Solved horizontally or vertically: There is one Helmet Shape facing upwards, one facing downwards and one facing right. There is one Dotted Fill, one Mottled Fill and one Right Slant Shaded Fill.
10) **d** - Solved horizontally: The top shape rotates 180°. The bottom shape flips horizontally.

PROGRESS CHARTS

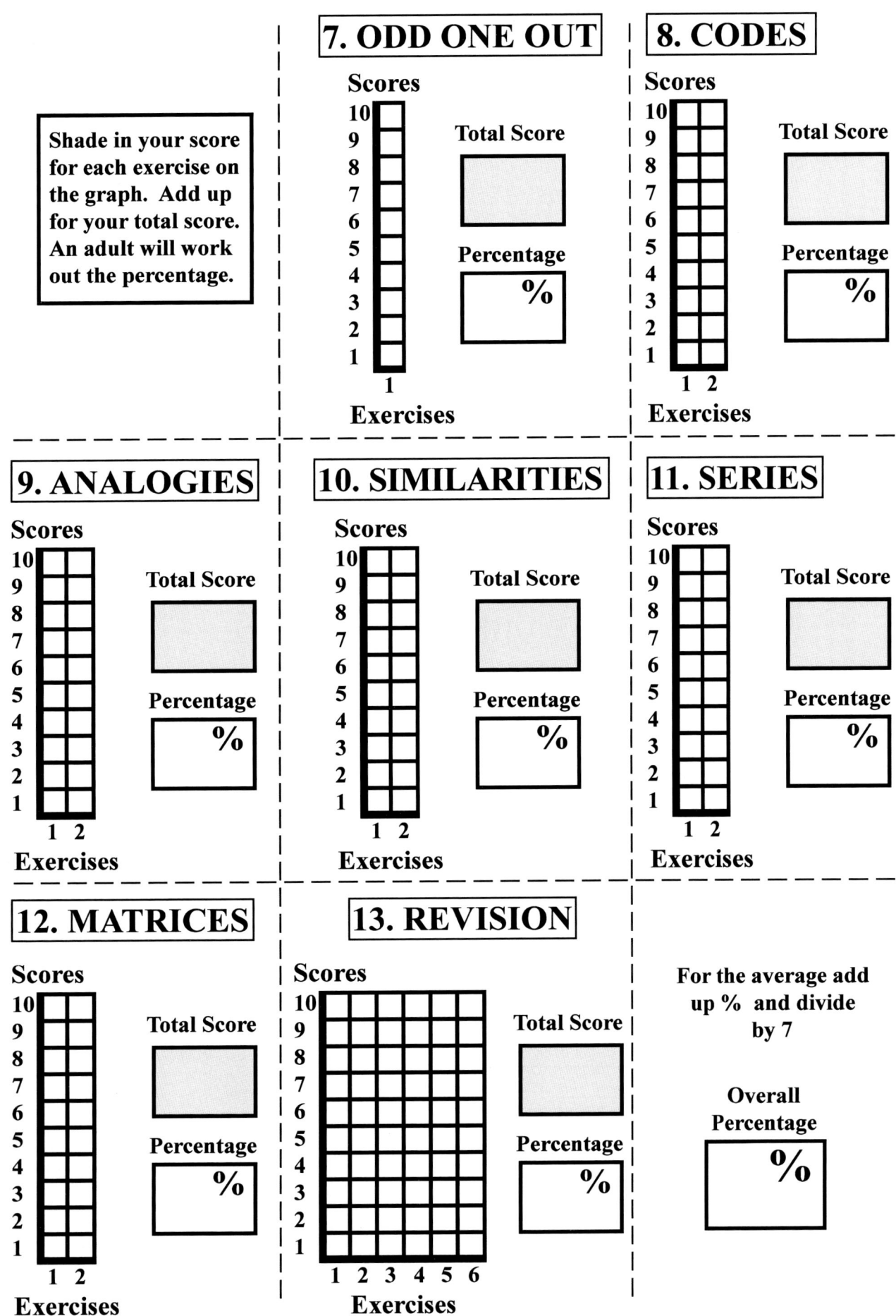

CERTIFICATE OF
ACHIEVEMENT

This certifies

_____

has successfully completed

11+ Non-verbal Reasoning
Year 3/4
WORKBOOK 2

Overall percentage score achieved [ ] %

Comment _____
_____

Signed _____
(teacher/parent/guardian)

Date _____